Spirits in the Classroom

A True Story of a Teacher's Adventures from Beyond

Jonny Angels

Grosvenor House
Publishing Limited

All rights reserved
Copyright © Jonny Angels, 2015

The right of Jonny Angels to be identified as the author of this
work has been asserted by him in accordance with Section 78
of the Copyright, Designs and Patents Act 1988

The book cover picture is copyright to Jonny Angels

This book is published by
Grosvenor House Publishing Ltd
28-30 High Street, Guildford, Surrey, GU1 3EL.
www.grosvenorhousepublishing.co.uk

This book is sold subject to the conditions that it shall not, by way of
trade or otherwise, be lent, resold, hired out or otherwise circulated
without the author's or publisher's prior consent in any form of binding or
cover other than that in which it is published and
without a similar condition including this condition being imposed
on the subsequent purchaser.

A CIP record for this book
is available from the British Library

ISBN 978-1-78148-342-8

In communication with an orb – Closer inspection reveals a face inside.

Contents

	Introduction	1
ONE	Awakenings	5
TWO	Spirits in My Dorm	16
THREE	Singapore - A Spiritual Encounter	30
FOUR	A Little Classroom Entertainment	42
FIVE	Marco's Communication: Dream or premonition?	52
SIX	The Vietnam connection	64
SEVEN	A Lost Brother from Beyond	75
EIGHT	Rest in Peace?	83
NINE	Contact On A Plane: Jewellery and missing items	92
TEN	In the Classroom: A Snake and a Crucifix	102
ELEVEN	Manila and Beyond	107
TWELVE	Tsunami	117
THIRTEEN	On the Road in, Rangoon, Burma (Yangon, Myanmar)	121
FOURTEEN	Pitfalls of Clairvoyance - Negative Experiences	132
FIFTEEN	Pet Angels	142
SIXTEEN	In the Staffroom –Hungarian Spirits say Hello	148
SEVENTEEN	Classroom Reflections	164

Introduction

If someone had ever told me in my youth that I would *become* clairvoyant or at least experience it, I would have said, "Excuse me? What did you say? Can you elaborate on that word 'clairvoyant'?"

Certainly, I hadn't expected anything of this nature to manifest particularly in my future years. Furthermore, it became more noticeable and prominent in the capacity of an English Language teacher within colleges and school classrooms, mostly in foreign countries. Well that's where my work took me since graduation at university and thereafter became an adventure, which I am still very much part of.

However, I knew, or rather 'felt' that I was using psychic abilities from gradual experiences but we are all unique and so it comes differently to all of us in this field. However, *Clairvoyance* – and the ability to feel, see and receive messages from spirit was something I thought happened to mysterious people who went into a trance and spoke in tongues or something more 'peculiar' of a similar nature. It was something which even I felt was creepy, and certainly up there on the 'oddball' list.

My story therefore, does not necessarily set out to explain my personal and comparative experiences between the abundance of TV psychics that are circulating around in the media.

This is however, my own personal and factual account of clairvoyant and related supernatural experiences mostly over the recent years. This is not a training manual for developing psychics but an honest, straight forward and personal account of some of those really unusual occurrences that I have encountered in my work and travels overseas, both inside and outside the classroom. I am not just in schools; I am out and about on the road in my free time. I use the word spirit throughout my story in the sense that the medium of communication comes from another source not explainable by scientific means – especially if you considered the odds of chance.

Yes, occasionally, unpredictably and often unintentionally within the classroom! This is the centre theme as this is where I just seem to notice it more as it became increasingly evident, although often at times, involuntary.

Let's make this clear first of all. I often use the term 'psychic reading' when often it can also be described as clairvoyant. One is directly linked to spirit and the other not necessarily so. In any case, the information is still passed on to the sitter from the unconscious via the medium/psychic.

As the saying goes, all mediums are psychic but not all psychics are necessarily mediums – and for which, I eventually got the initial and unexpected calling of a pure mediumship experience whilst overseas to a total stranger.

I switch between both psychic and clairvoyance, as on occasions it was not often known when experiencing such details – well in my case it wasn't! And for the most part, I prefer to call them spiritual readings because much of the information that was being confirmed by the recipient was related to 'dead' people. We can put it more discretely by saying those that had 'passed over'.

It maybe not new for the average psychic but when it is in the role of a teacher within a classroom and not having conscious awareness of the personal information I was receiving, then it was dynamic and could at times be emotional. I kept that emotional reaction inside and we have to detach ourselves particularly in situations like this.

As child however, I do remember sending 'mind reading' images to my friend next door and had a taste for adventure with ghost hunting days in alleged haunted houses as one does – particularly as a boy would like to do at that time. I was fascinated by magicians or illusionists as some of them call themselves these days and took my little magic book for kids to school. However, there was something lacking. The thirst for <u>real</u> magic, the real unknown, and the desire to touch the intangible and experience what others in their comfort zone would dismiss as scientifically implausible.

From my very early teenage years I had originally had an avid interest in UFO research. This fascination gradually dwindled as I came to my own conclusion at that time that the spiritual was more important than the physical. And so, thereafter I drifted into the realm of the spiritual leaving my obsession of UFO's (Unidentified Flying Objects) behind.

For me, I felt that the presence of other physical planetary life, we could never do much about anyway – in other words, I felt personally, the benefits to my life and others from direct spiritual phenomena and communication were likely to be more productive in my present physical lifetime.

There will be those skeptics and even those in the psychic profession who will quickly be able to give their own account, suggestions and an answer for these spiritual experiences. That is their viewpoint and prerogative, but this is mine.

This is a story of true experiences and adventures both inside and outside the schools and colleges as I discover the potentials of self-discovery along the way. One of my key attributes is to avoid egotistical readings, have a sense of humility and where possible, responsibility when dealing with serious and sensitive issues. However, it does not always go to plan as I describe later on in one or two attempted psychic readings!

And so, this leads me to describe a profound, remarkable and moving spiritual experience in detail for which I name it 'my awakenings'. It was indeed to be a *dynamic* awakening and much overdue, eventual self-realization of touching the spirit world. In other words, –a kick up the psychic butt to let me know it's real and not simply imagination! For too long, I had ignored the signs and now it was the time to be stirred.

I do try to focus on the angelic and by this I mean the light and not the dark although I get lectured from time to time that what I do or experience within this field of spiritual and psychic phenomena are not from the heavenly realm. I disagree with them on this.

However, I am not the only one who has been touched from spirit, but for me it has been a personal and life-changing, gradual process which can be obtained by most of us with effort.

I want to share part of it with you, as like yourself, I have felt myself to be just an ordinary person but for which we are sometimes termed a 'Sensitive'. Therefore, this is my account of my spiritual awakenings and experiences. It has felt good to let you know part of it. It has been even better for me to actually do something about it and finally record it.

Chapter 1

Awakenings

Sensitive in more ways than one, as a child, I grew up almost to the point of seclusion at one particular stage in my early teens. There was a point when I retreated into my own little world. Being also sensitive in the non-physical sense also reflected and heightened the effects of what was going on around me in the physical, everyday world. How I also perceived, felt and reacted to others around me was another matter.

I am sure there were many other children in this situation who were hypersensitive to ordinary social situations with people around us being the main focus and influence. At one stage as a child, I had sketched the word '*EXIT*' in huge block letters on my bedroom wall in orange and blue.

I often imagined walking into another dimension through the adjacent bedroom wall and into a place of enchanting mystery. When far away in a foreign land on my travels I fantasized being able to pop through an invisible wall of my hotel room and back into the former, homely little garden of my parents rather than have to take that frequent and arduous long-haul plane journey.

To think just how much fun that would be.

Then there was the drama from school years and beyond – Quite painful to fully describe. A flash-back, photographic memory with visions of violent bullying which I bore witness to and in some cases received, left indelible psychological marks. I had wanted superman or another angel representative of justice or strength to appear and beat the crap out of these obstreperous, ruthless and twisted individuals. The teachers seemed to be mostly oblivious, absent or conveniently busy elsewhere.

From the girls who stuck pins in the school goldfish so they floated to the bottom to the boys who chained helpless, weaker students to the railings during lunch-hour breaks when teachers were hidden away in their cosy staff-rooms – yes, it's all recorded in my crystal-clear memory just as most of us do from our own experience. But move on they say, forget the past. It is however, the past that moulds you.

Naturally, like others, I daily tried to avoid and survive with nerves intact during my youth. This developed into an emotional but empathetic nature towards those who may find themselves in the same situation growing up from what otherwise should have been the secure umbrella of observant tutors as protectors.

In and outside the school I *shared* the victims suffering but thought it was just a normal altruistic and humane sensitivity that anyone would feel to recall it in graphic, visual detail, as I am able to do so even today after all the years that have passed. Therefore, later in life, possessing enhanced empathy as a teacher, I was able to spot not only those of emotional need but also victims of one sense or another. Later as a teacher, I became vigilant for anything noticeable of a bullying nature with my heightened sensitivities now more established.

There will always be someone worse off than you, but both in and outside my school life as a sensitive human being I believe, expanded and contributed to my psychic awareness. It was already there, being nurtured. It was just boosted by my helplessness as an almost defenceless, innocent male pupil and perhaps at that time for my age, apparently weaker than other students in stature.

I felt every punch, kick, scream, tear and total submissive anguish and despair for those pupils who were used as torture tools for sadistic purposes in and outside school. To watch the perpetrators walk away Scot-free encouraged a plethora of dreams with a vengeance towards them. Where were you my angel? Where were you god? I thought, asked, quizzed and pleaded. Perhaps I was being watched and guarded from worse situations that could have been and for that, I have to be truly grateful. There is always someone worse off than us and I certainly witnessed it.

I often wonder who or what those former bullies, both male and female, later developed into.

Did they go on to have normal relationships, normal lives? Where are they now – and have they forgotten or conveniently erased and exonerated their memories?

Did they have a functioning and active spirit guide, which we are often told is protecting us as god's children and if so what were their guides up to? Were their guides defunct? I thought. Was their life-chart off course or their souls developing or in regression through hurting others? And then again was it related to karma at all? I was left with a myriad of questions to ponder.

I believe the spirit world did a significant amount of work to help me avoid worse situations that could have come about due to those monster-bullies. In effect, the spiritual guidance that I was unaware of at the time steered me clear of likely more severe situations that other unfortunate pupils been subjected to.

Of course, I can't prove that but my 'radar' was on full to survive. They may well have been lurking around the corner had I just walked blindly into them and thus, into the negative and helpless situation that would have ensued. These nasty and unruly characters, some from broken homes, were ready to ruin the rest of your life, not just your newly purchased school uniform.

As we know, childhood and school memories remain indelible and never leave you. As I ponder about the experiences which contributed to my own heightened, spiritual abilities I was also already more 'sensitive' than others to my surroundings – both social and environmental. And so therefore, neither have my memories and 'footprints' of the other spiritual dimension, left me either.

Scolded by spirit

If ever there could have been a newspaper heading *'spirit breaks up squabble in local household'* then I was a valid example of it. In my early teens, I clearly recall having an argument with my sister. We were in the living room and literally tearing each other's hair out over some simple issue as children do when in a rowdy squabble. My parents were not yet home from work as it was just a little after school closing time. I was thirteen and the argument was becoming quite vitriolic.

It wasn't uncommon for me to have an argument with my sister over some simple issue in those days but it was for it to become aggressive even by our sibling standards. Whilst in the middle of the rough and tumble, I suddenly sensed an almighty and resounding presence. It replaced normal words and feelings combined expressing a different kind of phenomena, whichI had never before recalled experiencing.

I heard and felt a resounding "STOP THIS RIGHT NOW!" more deafening and profound than a normal physical, audible sensation because of it being more than just one sense. I was able to not only know *who* it was but *what* the message was simultaneously. This voice came thundering and pulsating all through my body, in my head, my mind and consequently to my emotions which resulted in my swift, sharp response and reaction to immediately cease the squabble. I was only a kid and it was a shock.

A real shudder came over me as I was certainly shaken by the scolding effects. I retreated to an armchair in an adjoining room and nestled into it, where I remained motionless and certainly none the worse as if it had been a real verbal and physical scolding. It was indeed an unusual experience.

However, I immediately sensed it was my Aunt who had passed over at the untimely age of thirty due to a car accident five years previously. Why was I convinced it was my aunt? Because I felt, saw, and *knew*. It was what we call in the clairvoyant world 'The knowing' –or at least it sure was for me.

At that instant, of course my sister had asked me what was wrong for which I responded with a feeble and unconvincing 'nothing'. Can you imagine being in the heat of an argument and then suddenly your opponent swiftly withdrawing and even disappearing from the room without any rational explanation? Serves you right – that will teach you! You may say, but then an argument or disagreement has to take at least two.

Still, we are constantly told as children we have vivid imaginations and so it was not so difficult at that time to assume it was such and forget it, despite the intensity of it for me at that brief moment in time.

I am now certainly convinced that a spiritual explanation for this experience had manifested at that time. It took me several years before I realised that I was already picking up clairvoyant information. Besides that, coming initially from a strong Christian background, it was not particularly something to be acknowledged even if I had mentioned it. After all, children are frequently told that they have a vivid imagination anyway.

We also need to remember of those children whose stories were dismissed for describing events with clarity and frequency, which may have actually been about former lives. I am not talking about pixies at the bottom of the garden here but clear, detailed and concise information that the child could not have been prior exposed to, in any shape or form in their present lives.

And, so It wasn't until later in life, during my teaching career, it would seem frequent that I would sense which student's father or mother did what for a living by an unknown source. This could be brother, sister, aunts and uncles although not always definable which family member and whether they were still alive or not etc. This was not a conscious feeling and it was happening at random and it could have been whilst I was either writing on the whiteboard involved in my duties or addressing a student for a response to a question.

For example, sensing something tangible in the medical profession around the person's life would not always necessarily deem their parent or guardian to be a doctor but should certainly be connected to it. If I saw an image in my mind's eye of a white coat in picture formation it could not only be a doctor but anything from a pharmacist to any other occupation that may use the same uniform unless another subsequent more specific symbol clarified it more so.

However, it may be a link to a deceased relative's past career, in which case this puts a different dimension on the 'reading' as it could render it as coming direct from spirit communication instead of intuition or psychic. Remember, this is just my opinion and experience whilst others in this field may differ.

In my view, both abilities and senses are of a different consciousness in themselves and important to recognise although not always clear enough to the reader/psychic at the time.

Another typical example of clairvoyance I experienced was when I passed three recently closed-down shops in the local high street. These had ceased trading. I was not interested with the first two small shops, but for some reason I was VERY intrigued with the first one on the corner. I went back, stood outside the door, walked off but then came back. There was something going on here, which I could not pinpoint exactly so I decided to ask other shopkeepers both opposite and nearby. They informed me that the young owner had recently committed suicide due to accrued debts. How tragic that was. I had to ask myself whether his spirit made me pause there to ask fellow shopkeepers or just the energies and vibrations that made me anxious.

In The Classroom

The turning point however, became more noticeable and manifested itself more effectively for me in the school classroom whilst teaching. This was probably because I was now coming into contact with a larger number of groups of people including students and teachers that I was to work or teach with from a variety of nations and cultures. I have had the opportunity to teach a multitude of nationalities from Mongolians to Vietnamese including other Pan-Pacific students. I've also taught Arabs to Indians and Europeans in the UK.

In the initial stages, my psychic interaction was often involuntary and these clairvoyant experiences were only utilised in public outside later. I would be asked to do readings with angel cards or just approach those who I felt needed it with their permission.

Experts in the psychic world and later in the spiritual college in London that I attend insist you can control the gift with discipline but at the time in a class full of sometimes unruly and disrespectful students I was beginning to relish the benefits of the sixth sense to get their attention. However, I was still responsible enough to know when not to go too far with such spiritual information. On occasions, it was effective enough to result in a more disciplined class. Some of the students mistakenly felt I might occasionally be a mind reader, which caused ripples through the class to a few gasps of amazement at times. If they thought for example, their deceased grandparents were watching them they tended to become a little more attentive.

Depending on what culture and background they were from, I would of course get challenged. As one of my more skeptical students from China, folding his arms across his chest firmly, said "I don't believe!" in a rather stern but robotic tonation to affirm his fervent skepticism. That was ok, it didn't bother me and in any case, this would mean that if my psychic 'broadcasting' was mentioned to the boss, I could rubbish the idea as ever happening, insisting we were only playing a magician's trick too – ha!

However, regarding psychic phenomena, different cultures act differently to both spiritual beliefs and psychic practices, which often get exaggerated. I was just beginning to realise this negative viewpoint and hysteria by some of the teaching and reception staff at the workplace.

As a result and through time and experience I decided to tread carefully when admitting to any psychic information, ability or experiences to those who were likely to have a less favourable viewpoint, acceptance or understanding.

When to switch off? – That's another question – Life is full of surprises and it was just beginning to warm up.

One typical example would be where I could *feel* or *see* but not necessarily hear descriptions of my student's parent's professions, of family deceased or alive including descriptions of the locations surrounded in glorious or not so glorious colours. This could either be the interior or exterior of such property.

With certain students, just as I had put pen to the whiteboard with my back turned, I'd receive in my mind, words 'diplomat, pastor, policeman or even farmer, soldier' etc. It was sometimes just as if it could be heard over the shoulder but more often than not, I just knew it. From my experience, if the spirit related had to wear a uniform in their profession when they were alive then that would be the first visible item to show itself as clear as a shiny button.

One example I quite vividly remember involved viewing clairvoyantly the specific number of fifty horses of different colours swarming around one mature, Mongolian student as I addressed the class, taking the attendance register. Obviously I didn't count them in my mind's eye whilst simultaneously trying to teach but saw a flash of assorted running horses with the specific number. I was able to point out the favourite one with the white streak, which he proudly and enthusiastically confirmed, face in a full-beam smile.

These were confirmed by the relevant student. It wasn't until later on with an eventual trip to Mongolia that I witnessed how much the Mongolians grow up with horses. "You want a horse Jonny? ... and off they all galloped". Another video for my website, I thought. I declined their kind offer in view of their admirable horse riding skills compared with mine.

As a child I had been bitten by a horse and frequent nightmares of black or white stallions chasing me ensued for years. I have also noticed a few horses in my spirit photographs but being an animal lover that may be a contributing factor.

Meanwhile, as I entered the class for the first day and still in Singapore, I turned to my right and there was Dorj from Mongolia with a wide welcoming smile whilst Nancy, perked up in her chair like a sprightly, alert doll. "Welcome teacher," said Dorj in a sincere and respectful manner noticeably standing out from the rest of my noisy class of multi-national, Pan-Asian students.

As soon as I heard him speak I felt the word 'diplomat' come to mind in full clarity and he confirmed his father was indeed a diplomat, which I suppose may not be much of a big deal until you start to pick up further personal details of their dead relatives as I did on that day!

We got on with the lesson but I then felt the need to uncharacteristically say, "I tell you from this day, in this time, that I will be visiting your country in the near future". What had quite made me say that, I do not know but the sensing of the future event and experiencing it was similar to a déjà vu? It was just as real as if it were in the present moment and in effect, it flashed in front of me. I am sure many of us have experienced this.

On invitation, I did eventually visit my student's family and friends a few years later and thoroughly enjoyed doing angel card readings in the coffee bars and friend's homes, which were successful, never scathing and always amicable with a great sense of spirit, acceptance and atmosphere. Spirit Photography was something that developed later on with me and it was also in the hotels that I was able to get some strange spirit photographs both in the bar and in my room in Ulan Bator, the capital of Mongolia.

So, now with my teacher's hat off for the moment, I was well on the way to becoming more confident in this sixth-sense ability with the cards. I found that by beginning with psychic angel cards of immense glowing colours and artistic design, it opened up another door of the mind. Other images will emanate from the readers life as you read.

In the month of May a few years later, we met Dorj's close friends in a bar in Ulan Bator. I was already sensing specific, personal information about a father who had passed and was now warning him about making decisions in his life. Adding to this I had already captured a shadowy white face of a female in the corner of the bar on my camera and quite ostentatiously went about showing the bar staff the results. Unfortunately, one member of staff did not return to work ever again after that. I had gathered quite a bit of interest and curiosity as I showed them the photo of another large, Mongolian-looking face which was transposed clearly on the door of my room. That may have been part of the reason for the departure. I received quite a few uncomfortable looks after that occurrence within the hotel. They were never hostile, compared with some other cultures or people I had encountered on my travels regarding this subject matter. However, I am not so sure in the west whether we would take it so seriously even with the evidence unless of course, it happened to be direct poltergeist activity. On the other hand, it's possible some hotel proprietors would deny the existence of spirits in order to protect their trade. In their eyes, some guests wouldn't like this kind of phenomena regardless of whether there was evidence or witnesses. It may attract keen people like those of us interested in this phenomenon but not everyone.

Later one evening, Dorj's friend's took a group photograph with myself in it after forcing me to down a jug of Mongolian beer in one go to chants of "go Jonny, Go!". There was no escape from that, I tried and fortunately it wasn't Vodka which I certainly don't touch. On closer scrutiny of the photo with my new digital camera bought in Malaysia there was a distinct orb with a clear male face just above him, and nobody else. I talk more about orbs and spirit orbs later on, as this is another phenomenon that I like many, have experienced with intensity and prolific abundance in recent years.

I had a great time in Mongolia and surprisingly also had little problem finding vegetarian food in the main city of Ulan Bator. Surprisingly, I taught English to at least a couple of Vegetarian Mongolian students. One of them who sat in the front row of my class so I do think there have been some beneficial and surprising changes. This intrigued me since I was informed that livestock had outnumbered people 14 to 1, and yearly meat consumption reached around 200 pounds per person.

My room however, had no hot water and was still quite cold in the month of May as snow fell outside.

The bedroom was adorned in a kind of kitschy velvet maroon with some old-fashioned decor to add to the ambience. However, I felt there was something in here watching and orbs in the room began to appear. Later a large face appeared on the door, which I caught on camera and subsequently showed on my YouTube channel.

Chapter 2

Spirits in My Dorm

Being clairvoyant can lead to other unexpected occurrences. This, I had earlier stumbled across through my frequent travels overseas, but honestly hadn't become fully aware of the experiences for what they really were or their potential and implications.

As a former lecturer in a college for undergraduates also in Thailand, I had settled into my new campus, which was located in a plush setting in the tropical countryside, close to a golf course, at the base of the mountains. It was adorned with a well-managed landscape, exotic flowers and lush green tropical shrubs and palms. A white statue of an angel with a fountain made me feel at home, for a while.

Ironically – unless it was fate, it was exactly here that one year previously I had gone to visit the private college on a chance invitation by another teacher who was lecturing there from New Zealand. It was my weekend off, and I had travelled all the way from Bangkok by bus taking time off from my existing job there. I always have to get out of the city to relieve the stress of a full teaching load.

I had stopped to help him with his rental motorbike, which needed a push-start in the mid-day humidity and sizzling heat as I thought he was a tourist in need. In return, he had kindly invited me to go and take a look at the college he was teaching at and so I eagerly took up the offer of an informal visit at the drop of a hat. I also didn't want to miss the tropical countryside ride on a motorbike to pass the time getting there, as it was set in an isolated spot. The lanes within the vast college, set on a luxury golf course here, were also potentially snake territory, which I had witnessed a few times previously. I actually came face to face with a deadly one creeping down the curtains in my dormitory room after class had finished. I later learnt it was a venomous Viper. The security guard sorted that one out!

On arrival I was allowed to give myself a tour of the new, spacious college as my new acquaintance from New Zealand sorted out some paperwork in the office. I went off to explore the school and up a flight of whitewashed steps meandering through more spacious and empty corridors. It was college break so no students were there but it had quite a haunting atmosphere, so I thought.

A large, corner room found my attention. As a former active, musician I discovered a modern-looking piano in good working order, only a fraction out of tune with a melodic enough tone and with a reasonable pitch.

I can only describe the attraction for a musician just as a bee would search for pollen which suddenly found a brightly coloured flower –except the piano was gloss white in an empty but cavernous room, with a couple of chairs and a desk.

I sat down, and as I usually do, immediately began to play a very popular ballad that was once number one the world over for a famous iconic, musician and singer from Liverpool. I played it in timely fashion to the traditional slow but steady rhythm. I never have forgotten the chords or words and played it to the exact key and style as when I was a child. Being inspired by one of the all-time best selling artists of the century, then you can take the hint. A simple song and piano ballad yet it evokes wonderful emotion and the words do have a spiritual meaning of the afterlife in my opinion.

I have always felt there was something haunting but wonderfully spiritual about the sound and song *'Imagine'* including the lyrics or both. I had also often felt there was some other divine help assisting me when playing it alone on this occasion.

I had once recorded my own compositions in a recording studio and was complimented by a former successful musician with the descriptive words – *hypnotic* and *spiritual* for my own material. I never did pursue my musical career despite achieving local and regional radio stations airing and two chat interviews. This was under a different name of course. It was later that I used my musical aspirations in the classroom to inspire the students instead.

I recall at home whilst a child, having played *'Imagine'* several times. I played it over and over by ear to heart so much. A few days later I awoke from sleep feeling as if I was 'floating' in the middle of the room and slightly higher than the top bunk bed. Possibly due to the shock of this I immediately landed with an almighty thud from my top bunk bed onto the floor. Nobody was using the bottom bunk, but was reserved for my absent brother at that time.

I am not exactly saying I had involuntarily levitated fully awake or even in half-awake stage, but that it certainly felt like it. This was what I was experiencing moments before I was abruptly knocked senseless from the crash to the ground. Oh, and no, I never have taken hallucinatory drugs or ever would. As I was 'floating' around the room, playing repeatedly in my head was that very same song. I had now been literally levitating –or so it felt and seemed, across the room in some kind of altered consciousness. There was a bang on the door at 3 am. It was my mother "Jonny, are you all right? I hope you aren't hypnotizing yourself or something" This was probably on the assumption that all the books I had read and 'strange' groups I had joined, such as UFO research during my childhood were probably to blame.

Meanwhile, here I was now in this newly built college in Thailand, formerly known as The Kingdom of Siam surrounded by freshly whitewashed walls, and tall pillars. I sat at the piano thinking of that wonderful song, it was now ingrained in both my conscious and unconscious.

I was sitting composed, calm and alone with a view of the hills and a splendid, gushing fountain of water. Quite appropriate I thought, the lyrics from the song, whilst I gazed at the clear blue sky with a few fluffy, white clouds through the wide, campus window. It did indeed make me want to reflect on life in a spiritual way. I said to myself whispering with a passionate plea, 'spirit guide, angel, I would truly love to work and live here'. These words of mine suddenly came from the heart and there was something that felt I should be right here at this moment and be a special part of it. I have often spoken to god or a guide, or you may want to call it an angel or whatever. This was regardless of any evidence for me at that stage.

The atmosphere in the room felt uplifting and I felt vigorously intuitive and I thought why not try? It may be worth it with nothing to lose. I quickly and distinctively felt some kind of spiritual vibes too, not just in the room but also throughout the whole college. At the time I was not aware of what the actual reason was for this. Furthermore, I truly felt that I was not alone here, despite the college being closed for vacation and end of semester. This was surely an inspiration and another good reason to sit and play the piano with emotion, privacy and with passion.

It wasn't until later I had discovered the area had once been used for a movie related to the infamous 'Killing Fields' of Cambodia but in this case it wasn't so much negative vibes I was feeling, just that here and unusually for me, I felt that there was someone else in the room. Astoundingly, One year later, I responded to an advertisement for the job at this very college, which I had spotted in the national newspapers by chance. We have heard the phrase, 'coincidences, of which there are none'. This case may have been true.

I enthusiastically went for the interview which took four to five hours by bus – at that time two hours of arduous traffic jams just to get through the notoriously congested city of

Bangkok to the other side and a further six hours to get to my final destination by a separate long-distance bus journey. Transportation has improved there now, but it still can get quite jammed at rush hour, weekends and public holidays.

I was fortunate enough to be accepted for the job as lecturer by a panel of wise-owl academics sitting in plush armchairs around a large polished, oval teak business desk. They all appeared to be wearing academic-looking, formal glasses including a mature, moribund Thai woman of matronly appearance who was wearing a gold monocle on a chain with chubby red cheeks. She seemed to have two jobs – one as Chief Librarian and the other as Matron of the college. However, I was ecstatic to be called for the interview–the low salary didn't matter. I just wanted to get away from my previous sweatshop-school in the smoke-choked city teaching English. It could be arduous and stressful although I have some fond memories of my classes and students.

On arrival at the new college I knew exactly where I wanted to go and arrived early. I immediately made my way through the grand new hall and up the stairs to the same room with the glossy, white, polished piano. I sat down on the piano stool, which was neatly tucked under it in the same spot as I had exactly done so less than one year previously. I gently placed my fingers to the keys, began to sing and played with passion and emotion *Imagine* all over again in the same empty, pristine whitewashed room.

Not that this was the only composition I was able to play as a previous musician – it just felt the right thing to do as if I was paying some kind of spiritual homage with a 'thank you'. Just at that moment the door opened slowly and ominously with a creaky-hinge noise; it was now fully ajar.

I immediately stopped playing, a little startled, got up and went to greet whoever maybe there but there was nobody. I closed it and then carried on playing for just a few more moments. For me, it was clear there was certainly a feeling of something going on here; maybe a spiritual atmosphere in the building, but it was only just beginning to unfold. If only I knew what was coming.

Meanwhile, I felt the spiritual vibes again; I will call it a *sixth sense* but there was certainly something here. Large, empty classrooms ready to be used whilst the international but mostly pan-Asian students were still being recruited. Recently whitewashed walls and corridors I couldn't help thinking I was being watched. I didn't know *what* it was I was feeling, but it was clear it was something intangible but not of the physical.

My attention was immediately drawn to a colourful wooden, hand-made spirit house at the entrance of the college as I entered the wide college gates. These are not so common in the west of course but in many countries of the Far East and Asia they are an integral part of their culture, religion and tradition. On the college bus I asked the matronly, head librarian what the purpose of this small, golden structure was. Her tone immediately changed as she sighed in a melancholic way. Her expression softened and became sullen, her monocle shifting slightly as she squinted and twitched her eye. She told me how five students had been killed in less than two years due to the poor road conditions and dangerous driving. So they had erected this spirit house just after their deaths as a remembrance not just for traditional reasons.

I was shocked. Did she say five students? I pondered this. All killed in less than twelve months? What about their families? Oh God, I thought as I felt an ache in the pit of my stomach. Had the college forgotten them completely and the rest of the students just avoided the issue?

It certainly made me pause to think that these students had only recently and actively been present in these classrooms that I was to begin teaching. The thought filled me with emotion and sorrow remained. Why doesn't anyone say anything? I glumly thought, feeling uncomfortable that I had raised the issue of the spirit house. What is it about 'death' that people find difficult to talk about – after all, these were real, living breathing people in the physical with everything to live a happy and successful life for.

They were also most likely, bright and cheerful undergraduates that were contributing to the social life of the college and preparing for their life ahead and sat next to some of those I will soon be teaching. We can describe them as gone from the physical but that doesn't mean we or they, don't miss each other despite being in the other dimension.

Tragedy affects hearts and minds and I believe they were frozen in time where these students left their last memories. After all, people had died and families had been shattered. If I hadn't asked about the spirit house, then I may not have known until much later, or not at all. Or so I thought.

Meanwhile, I decided to take a walk to the end of the long, winding and spacious driveway at the college entrance to visit the spirit house. There was a gentle breeze despite the humidity amongst the lush, green tropical shrubs and trees. This little shrine intrigued me. I certainly felt drawn to it and wondered why others weren't as much as me. These spirit houses are often but not always, small doll's house size in appearance and put in place for respect when someone has died, or to serve as protector of the property.

In these small spirit houses are often placed items such as little statues of elephants adorned with fragrant, incense holders, candlesticks, and vases for flowers of different assortments. With my visit to the little spirit house, one could be forgiven for thinking it was a morbid fascination but my interest in this instance was one of empathy too and not merely inquisitiveness. I also distinctively felt some kind of pull to this spot. Despite the fact that I have always taken an interest in antiquated cemeteries as a child and as an adult too I do feel some kind of spiritual attraction. I lived around cemeteries for quite a while and still do visit them.

The Prayer

This spirit house visit was also my idea and opportunity to pay my respect for the small group of young students who had passed over less than one year earlier in vehicle crashes on the hectic and dusty main road.

I made sure there was nobody around when I visited as it was late in the evening, although I was vaguely aware of being watched from a far distance by one of the guards, but that was ok as I was a lecturer and not an intruder but they do still get rather suspicious or at least curious of our movements. They can be quite keen to exercise their authority when in a uniform. I wandered past the college fountains. As I approached all I could hear was the croaking of the tropical bullfrogs in the swampy but lush undergrowth around me on the perimeter of the college.

At the spirit house, I held out my pre-written prayer and began to pray whilst speaking out aloud but just slightly audible for obvious reasons and said;

"Hello, I am Jonny, The new lecturer here – Look, I am so deeply sad that you had to go and leave us so soon. I never knew you personally and it is so unfortunate that you couldn't complete your studies here at the college.

I know you didn't expect it to happen and such a tragedy will not be forgotten, least of all by me. But, I am a new lecturer here and I wished that I could have had the chance to have met and teach you so I pray now for your souls and hope you can move on.

I am so very sorry for your early passing. I pray for you, your families and your precious friends – some of who may still be here at the college. I know that each time I pass this spot at this spirit house I will never, ever forget what happened to you and will remind others not to forget too."

It upset me to think that these students, full of vitality like all the other fresh faces around had come a long way from their homes or countries overseas to complete their studies. They had of course, expected to do so, but now they were suddenly gone. I mean, in the prime of their life, full of encrgy, hope and aspirations and then –'curtains'. How can we expect a grieving family to rest? How can we expect an active spirit to either?

At the time, I was teaching day-to-day as a Media arts lecturer for undergraduates; a subject quite different to my usual English language teaching. I had been thrown into the deep end and was very much on my own, which naturally lecturing in an international College differs to a Language school. Of course, I had my own podium and all the other technical equipment to go with it including the elevated stage – yes a stage, or more like a raised platform! Ironically, very similar to those that mediums use in spiritualism colleges.

It could be seen as useful in times of theatrics and drama to stress a teaching point, or alternatively render myself an embarrassment when one of the international students, particularly from Europe decided to challenge me. Slightly elevated, facing a crowd of students who may be eager to learn or not, could sometimes be daunting if I hadn't prepared enough lesson material the days before. As for being positioned from the podium, slightly elevated on the lecturing platform, It was only later I realised I was picking up vibes, personal information from my students.

As for the former students who had tragically lost their lives on the roads outside the college, I had truly wondered with empathy what it must be like to be the parents who lost their children. After all everyone assumes them to be in a safe and secure environment. How tragic that they didn't realise about the dangers of the roads and driving in this part of Asia.

Dormitory spirit

The following night, during sleeping hours in my temporary, dormitory room on campus, I was suddenly and abruptly awoken by what I thought initially was simply just a bad shaking dream. You know the one where the bed shakes uncontrollably. I mean just that – shaking physically as if I was being held by the shoulders and vigorously pushed back and forth. If you have seen what is sometimes done to a person who has passed out, where someone shakes them rigorously, attempting to revive them then you get the idea.

However, on abruptly awakening it wasn't just a dream at all. I was awoken by an intense jolt as if someone was grabbing me to deliberately and intentionally wake me up, quite urgently to get my attention. It certainly worked, that's no underestimate!

The bathroom light was on, door slightly ajar with just enough light to be able to get up and walk around without bumping your head or knee. I had been in a deep sleep then suddenly shaken. I opened my eyes and there in front of me, as clear as day, a young face a few inches from my nose! A student I thought? For God's sake! I recognized that uniform and collar. "What are you doing here? How did you get in?" I said. But within seconds he was gone and fizzled away into thin air.

It may sound far-fetched as if I am describing Caspar the ghost but that was really it. I will not forget that face. Fresh-faced and full of vitality with pale, Chinese or Thai features and tone, as clear as day in a college uniform top. I immediately got out of bed and went to my door extremely disturbed by the experience.

There was no need as the door was firmly locked and bolted of course. In any case, what was the point, I now knew what I saw – a spirit, which awoke me at 3am precisely then disappeared from my vision into thin-air on awakening. It was most certainly too real to be an ordinary dream. Or was it just a dream? I had already woken but the spirit and image was still there in front of me although briefly, it was vivid.

If I hadn't seen someone or something for real, I certainly would not have called out to request, "who the hell are you?" – That's for sure! It *was* so unmistakably real; I am describing it as best I can here. I recall clearly the expression on his face was a mixture of distress as well as some kind of intrepid inquisitiveness but certainly not threatening at all.

In less than a few seconds I was able to see and sense that whoever woke me was either coming to check me out, perhaps get me to do something or go somewhere for assistance. At least, it was for attention. Perhaps it was intuition again or feelings and words unspoken from spirit. At 3 am in the morning I was being drawn back to the spirit house at the gates – but I wasn't going anywhere at that time of the morning hours! I had to teach a class at 8:30 am anyhow.

In the early days of my spiritual awakenings however, I was not aware of spiritual messages and I now feel this was an attempt of deliberate communication. The experience was too real to be just an empty ghost vision. In my opinion this was an active spirit-personality and just as if someone is face-to-face, eye to eye in the flesh minus the smell of breath. If you have ever been in a country when someone suddenly grabs you by the wrist and asks you for money or help, then you should be able to visualise the impression, except it wasn't hostile.

Meanwhile, at the college, in the morning word got around that I had seen something in my room in the dormitory on the ground floor. My room was at the end of the corridor but still on the student's campus. I was in temporary accommodation and due to be moved to lecturers quarters the following week.

On my way to class in the corridor, one of my Thai-Chinese students approached me eagerly, with a wide-eyed look. He asked me if it really was true that I had seen a ghost that night. Where was it? Who did the ghost look like? I pondered for a moment why he would say 'who?' rather than 'what?' it looked like.

Suddenly his face changed and mouth dropped open. As I described where it happened, which specific room I witnessed it in and what the spirit looked like, my student gasped and looked shocked.

He went onto explain that it was the very same room where he and his Chinese roommate had been sharing before his death. I felt another cold chill down my spine. He persisted, asking me to describe him for further clarification, which I did. By now there was a small crowd of students gathering around me as I clutched my batch of books for the morning lecture, trying not to drop them. He was perturbed by hearing about my experience more than I was. After class, I decided to head down to the student affairs office to ask to see the previous year's college photos.

I held my breath. Confirmed! The student in my dorm was in the photo and just as I had seen him in my room with the abrupt awakening at exactly 3am. There was only one photograph of him as the secretary informed me all of their possessions and other memorabilia had since been removed by the parents. As I scrutinised, matched and re-confirmed the student I had seen in the photograph, it made me immediately think back and link my recent visit to the spirit house and the prayer which I had written and read from my heart. What had I started at the college as I sang and played the song *'Imagine'* in an empty, perhaps haunted room?

Later, I was cautioned by the vice president about 'scaring' students with 'false stories' and so naturally had to tone down the whole affair pretty much swiftly. I do not know how it got back to the President of the college who sat in his Ivory tower but it certainly did somehow.

I didn't change my dormitory room as I was not troubled too much myself. I was just perturbed that night by something unusual that I had not been familiar with before compared to normal 'dreams'.

I wouldn't say I was scared by the visitation but was most certainly wondering if it would occur again.

Next evening, I decided to return to the little spirit house one more time and what ensued, actually happened:

At around 11pm on the weekend when most of the students had left the college and their dorms, I approached the spirit house one more time.

I spoke again from the heart.

"I know you are here and that one of you visited me last night. I thank you for accepting me and wanting to contact me here. I understand your heartache, shock and loss but I really believe that you should move on, go to the light and move on."

I know some may think that little message was so spiritually cliché but as a spiritual newcomer at that time, it was the only idea I could muster which came straight from the heart again. Besides, I didn't want loose spirits spooking me out in my new job at the end of a dark corridor or back in my college dormitory, did I? This place was huge and rather empty, particularly at night. Most weekends the college was deserted except for a few security guards at various points through the vast college acres and meandering countryside lanes.

As I moved away from the spirit house just after saying another prayer, I walked a few feet around the corner and something startled me by surprise. I nearly fell off the college-grounds curb. A large bird with a streak of black and white plumage, and about the size of a gull dropped from the air above barely missing my shoulder and feet by inches. It landed with a great whack onto the pavement in front of me. Adding to this, its eye was seemingly, aiming ominously right at me as blood trickled from the corner of its beak. Remember, this was late evening and not during the hot daytime period.

Of course the bird was now sadly dead and had died just this moment but was still warm. I had never experienced this before and it only just missed my head by a split second.

However, it was not just the sudden, startling drop and noise of the bird plopping at my feet from the tree above but the actual timing of it. I love animals and seem to have a strong rapport with them. However, this was a mystery, an unfortunate but apparently healthy looking bird that happened to mysteriously drop out of the sky 30 seconds after I had just finished a visit to the 'deceased at the little spirit house following a prayer.

We can come to our own conclusions about this experience but it would be comforting to know that spirit had nothing to do with it. Who knows? Perhaps negative, so called 'residual energies' were so strong as if to be influential, which just couldn't move on and wanting to be heard. I had later been told by an Indian friend of a Yogi Organisation in Kathmandu, Nepal that, "I had released the soul of a spirit and the unfortunate bird was the result of it" –but of course I cannot be sure of this, it's just speculation.

Up to that time and most of my life I had believed 'ghosts' to be things that are exactly that, ghostly images with semi-transparent bodies that walk through walls and don't recognise those of us being in their space. Indeed, I was led to believe that they were probably energy images of what was long gone and had no abilities to communicate let alone think.

It seems I was wrong in this particular case. I have since learnt there are those of us who can experience full-bodied spirits – those spirits that appear to us as being real and we would not know the difference. Only later did we realise there was something odd about it that just didn't add up.

Similar to clairvoyance, one can feel much more than a normal spoken, single sentence of communication –you may receive the spirits personal feelings, the question and the message all at the same time. This is something I have since learnt from experience and later, training. In fact dreams are of similar substance except this wasn't a dream as I had already woken up. I often wonder how many of us are not aware that we are in active communication with spirit, under the assumption it was just a vivid but unusual dream. Anyone remember seeing a person at the foot of their bed whilst waking-up during the middle of the night for seemingly no reason? Then you switch on the light and they're gone. Some seem to dismiss it as just a dream, which probably makes them feel more comfortable about it.

Chapter 3

Singapore – A Spiritual Encounter

A few years after working in Thailand, I flew to Singapore to begin a teaching post. This hot and humid island is at the bottom half of the Malaysian mainland and was once a former British colony until its independence in 1965. It's mostly a mixture of Chinese, Malay and Indian with Tamil, which makes it an interesting blend.

However, it wasn't long before I began to feel more than just a cultural experience but more of the spiritual. I suddenly experienced an abrupt spiritual wake-up right here in my hotel. For me, it was another profound experience of the afterlife, which took me by surprise. This was it, I thought. This was the spiritual moment I had long been waiting for, but not really expecting. I checked into a budget hotel in The Little India area, settled into my tiny room that I had already moved to from another room due to the rapacious and rampant bed bugs in the previous one.

I had spent half the night at this place with an electronic mosquito racket pulverising at least one bloated bed bug that had attempted to sink its vampiric and parasitic 'teeth' into me. I actually burnt a hole in the bed sheet that night with that racket. It was one of those hotels. Thank goodness, I have moved on since then and have gone upmarket. I had booked and paid for a room for the week at this place! Arriving on a weekend in Singapore could be a problem if you arrive after 6pm so this place was the only option at the time. Fortunately, the hotel changed hands later, has been totally revamped and much improved since then.

As I lay on the bed I briefly glanced towards an antiquated, cracked stain-glass window with a medium-size hole. There was an irritating leaking tap feeding a puddle, slowly advancing towards my bed from the adjoining 'en suite' bathroom. It was the last single room available so no chance of changing. I got out my spiritual book from my baggage. At this stage I hadn't even bothered to study the spiritual subject of channeling. Nothing to do with TV sets here – this is the other world 'channel' as in mediumship!

However, I just kept picking it up and flicking idly through a few pages. Not being one for disciplined meditation exercises, I kept reading so far and putting it down and picking it up for a read during the afternoon and evening. I put the book down, left my room and wandered down the steep flight of aging stone stairs, which are quite common in older Chinese-Asian buildings. They have the type of steep staircases that are enough to break your neck if you slip and that's without even trying.

I thought to myself they must have had Ghurkha mountaineers in mind when they built these never-ending staircases. The same can be said for the flights of steps that approach the temples. Meanwhile, each time I passed the pleasant and courteous middle-aged, Chinese-looking receptionist at the bottom of these steep stairs, I felt as if her face was familiar. I certainly wasn't sure what it particularly was that gave me the feeling I may know something about her. It was certainly puzzling me.

I thought at first it was her amicable, gentle personality that made me feel I *should* approach her, but what I was supposed to say, goodness knows. Of course, I didn't really know her and I had never met let alone been in Singapore before at that time.

She told me her name was Lana and she was not originally from Singapore. Up to this time this is all I actually knew about her, as I had just booked in and am not the kind of person for being gregarious with hotel staff on the first day.

The second day of my stay however, the feeling got a little more intense as if I *must* say something to her but I was not aware of what. Again I passed her sitting behind the reception desk and smiled courteously, in a slightly inquisitive manner, just as she was attending to incoming migrant worker guests. I handed my room-key across the counter still feeling something spiritually alluring as well as peaceful, but which to me was not so normal.

Next day, evening as usual, Lana the receptionist was on the evening shift again. I felt the need to go downstairs and make my way to the adjacent open-street bar to go to drink and enjoy a glass of soya-bean milk. I had put my book down on the subject of Channeling and Mediumship and left it spread open on the bed, centre pages. The chapter was quite clearly about communicating with spirit, which I hadn't yet completed.

Now in the tiny foyer of the little hotel, this time the feeling that I should speak to the receptionist about something specific was now so considerable and intense. I walked past, stopped halfway on the stairs and simultaneously felt and saw in my mind this hazy-pink mist beginning to emanate from her aura where she sat busily attending her bookkeeping behind the counter.

I felt as if I was standing in a fluffy cotton-wool cloud, in such spiritual awe and atmosphere that this time I could no longer resist asking her some personal questions. I was now, what seemed to me being *physically* drawn to the reception desk, almost like a magnetic effect and as if literally being pushed.

She was busily serving customers and exchanging the cash at this hectic budget hotel and it didn't seem I could resist the 'push' despite the small queue of guests who were now hassling her about the price of a room for three persons and trying to get a discount. She briefly looked over her glasses at me then back to her accounts books and troublesome guests, as she vehemently explained there was no discount. However, she was aware I was there. There was a small portable TV on the counter, which was audible but slightly annoying and distracting.

However, although being aware of her current working predicament I couldn't resist the spiritual pull and there didn't seem any other way out of this. I decided to go for it and say what I felt. I immediately asked Lana if she was aware that she had a very strong *spiritual presence* around her. She chuckled in a friendly, amused way as if not so overtly interested. Just then I could feel something heavy, black and sticky across my chest something similar to a tar substance you'd see on the roads but I *knew* it was on the chest just like thick treacle.

I asked if she had anyone in the family who passed over with a problem starting from the chest and up to the neck – I could feel wheezing and it seemed like smoking as I could sense the smoke – I was being shown clouds of tobacco smoke now in my mind. I placed my hand across the throat area to emphasise to her. I now not only sensed an older female, but also saw the clear face in my mind's eye quite clearly as one would do so when being handed an old photograph of a relative. The smile was soft and affectionate.

Letting out a short gasp, Lana promptly confirmed, with eyes now widening and glazed, that her mother had died of cancer and it was lung related. She paused as she held her pen in a slightly agitated way but asked me to continue with a faint but polite, approving smile. Then, with the speed and flow of running water the personal details came through one after another, such that I found challenging to keep up with it. Tears welled up in her eyes as she cautiously asked me to continue with bated breath as if her heart was skipping a beat and so was mine.

The remaining disputing, migrant-worker guests were now keeping quiet out of curiosity, fascination or maybe even discretion. By now they had edged away but kept on staring with intrigue from a dark corner of the narrow space-challenged lobby at the top of the stairway, where we were all standing. I felt now that I couldn't just cut off this opportunity due to a few loitering guests and besides I wasn't at the Hilton.

She paused with some trepidation and wonder at the consistent and validated information, enquiring how I could possibly know, for which I had no feasible answer at that moment in time. Lana handed me some notepaper, as I now had to have a pen in hand whilst trying to handle the constant flow of facts whilst simultaneously trying to control the speed of information. This was done whilst she was serving other guests who had arrived at the busy reception counter at the top of the stairs. All of this carried out unlike normal reception areas, which are more often than not located on a ground floor.

As the receptionist became emotional she wiped another tear from her eye, informing me that she had never got over was her parents passing. Of course we can't get over death and many of us may only manage to get through it. Standing at the reception desk, all of this information was trying to inundate me with facts and figures, images and descriptions of people and places, dates and times. It was like surfing a wave for which I had no means of finding any brakes or a wave that kept coming in and out with the tide.

This *was* my spiritual awakening. This was regardless of there being customers around and a noisy, soiled portable TV on the counter next to me. I seemed to have been able to block all that off and was being helped from spirit.

I was aware about mediums breathing more effectively to control the flow and energy of spirit communication but even at this stage I was not sure if it was psychic or total clairvoyance sensing spirit. I asked for the flowing information to be slowed down and I was soon able to identify that it really was spirit. I was of course elated. There was pure elation at what I had just been able to share with spiritual assistance and by now Lana was beaming, with tears of joy, but still confused as well as deeply curious where and how I was receiving the personal but welcoming information. She also confirmed she was Catholic, which I had already picked up on that information via spirit. I saw clearly *both* her deceased mother and father. I asked her to further confirm that her father had a much darker complexion than her mother and his name was Harry.

He was up there in front of me like a hanging, multi-dimensional TV screen image. I was now being shown a much cherished and large old wooden boat. "Tell her about the boat," came the rapid thought, like bullet-speed but gentle enough to feel as a clear spiritual whisper.

I described his dark-blue mariner's hat with a badge and a 'Siris' – that was the exact name of his old wooden boat that he nicknamed after Osiris an Egyptian god. I was able to describe the building it was kept in and where, as I followed the images and held onto them. Of course she was as stunned as I was and I realised by now that I was receiving active spirit information – and it was evident that the communication was intended with one of love and compassion, as well as concern for her daughter.

There was the unmistakable feeling – a strong sense of compassion as I stood there trying to hold the energy link as best I could with such mental manoeuvring. Lana shed some more tears as the information from her parents in spirit poured out, but she didn't want me to stop now. I paused only briefly to ask her if she had any questions. I struggled to hold on to the energy-link of information as I simultaneously tried to keep up with writing down in note form the salient points of information, whilst holding onto the image of her parents. She said she had no questions as she told me she "felt I had known her all her life" which was a little bizarre. But then considering the rare and consistent, personal information, which was pouring out that was understandable.

Probably she felt this way due to the fact I had, with spiritual assistance, just revealed most of her life through specific, private and personal detail, which I was moved by too. It was precise to her and evidential. This I cannot be clearer about, perhaps she meant it in the spiritual sense. I had never met her before and had no detailed knowledge of Indonesia either. I felt at this stage that it was part of a healing process for her to receive all of this evidence. Her deceased parents were doing their best to show her they were not dead, as in gone forever. After all, Lana admitted one of the hardest parts of her life had been accepting her parents had died.

Of course, we know that it is not death, as we know it that we are dealing with and so this is why I use, like many, the term 'passing over' and this is generally understood. And for sure, she was soon to be converted as before our own eyes pure facts in detail describing her family life both past and present were rolled out to see. I will never forget the image of the flowers in her parent's front garden that were conveyed to me. They were so vivid and radiant and I can still 'see' them now.

I have to say that I am also a rational person and equally cautious when approached by those with psychic abilities, as I always wanted to experience and see for myself first hand. I got my answer in this case, and so did Lana despite being staunchly catholic.

What was I to make of the crystal clear image of her father's face seemingly hanging in the air above Lana with a beaming smile? I was able to clearly sense the tone of his complexion, so detailed and graphic and as much as any material photograph could convey. This is all truly a blessing. I can't forget the glowing, radiant smile from both the mother and father, which emanated love and compassion as well as concern for their daughter in an almost angelic intensity. I saw her father in a crystal clear photo frame smiling down on us. This will always be indelible in my mind and still is up to this day. I believe it was her deceased mother who was projecting the images to me clearly as she was the more prominent of the two and appeared first. I was able to describe the wheelchair, the beautiful yellow and blue flowered dress that she had actually passed over in.

As Lana confirmed to me that she was a Catholic I was able to mention the name of her hometown in Surabaya, Indonesia from where her mother was also. All of this information had to come from somewhere and someone and I had just been given the rare opportunity to pass it on. I was able to pass on the name of the Pastor at the local church in her village and the specific gifts they had given to him including that which her mother had made – she liked to make specific cakes using dates and local citrus fruits.

At first I thought I was making this up. How could it be true? It was one fact after another and no vague possibilities or other self-doubt. And considering up to this stage in my development I had read about others doing such readings, but did not expect it to be me!

Initially, I was actually shaking a little as I steadily held my nerve and connection for the first stage of the opening reading. I was surely being helped by some divine guidance, I thought. Think about it – I was telling a complete stranger about her parents, her family and life from the year she was born and I had no way of knowing why it was so. The feeling of concern and love for their daughter was profound and moving and that encouraged me to continue. It wasn't only my day – it was Lana's for sure and I had to allow this life-time opportunity for her mother to come through too for which I was not resisting either!

I began to get 'Mira'. "Yes!" she said ecstatically, "that's my daughter".

I was shown the city of Berlin and an art college, and the fact that her daughter had changed the colour of her hair and had sent her a photo the previous week. "Is this correct?" I said.

She beamed widely as she told me her daughter was studying at a design college in Berlin and laughed in astonishment as she had indeed coloured her hair to a rather ostentatious pinky-red.

"Well, seems there's a flight being prepared –you are thinking of it?" I said confidently and swiftly as the information flowed effortlessly. I was beginning to enjoy this flow.

Lana was indeed in the process of planning a flight but wasn't sure whether she could make it. I felt she wouldn't but I didn't mention it.

With all this on-going flow of information from beyond the grave (or the heavens depending on your viewpoint) my emotions were also touched and I felt drained but no doubt this was due to energy depletion involved.

Why I was chosen I am not so sure, unless particularly the mother in spirit was waiting for the right time and person with the ability to walk into her daughter's place of work. This was an *ability* for which the true potential I was not fully aware of at that time. I happened to be reading a spirit book on channeling, which had been opened and clear to see on my bed in the small hotel room I was in. So if spirit was watching, it made sense to attempt a more suitable contact and opportunity. It just happened to be me.

I continued to do whatever readings I could for Lana over the next few days or so. I would even rush straight from my school after classes to get a message for her. At times when I was preparing to go back to the hotel from school I would just sense the thought which would say "Jonny, don't rush, she's not there". It was effective enough to influence my actions. And surely enough, on arriving at the hotel I would find she was not working on that shift.

On the last day of the continuous and successful on-going readings, the message and feelings I received from the deceased parents were that the man she was now in a relationship with and apparently married to was not a pleasant one at all and was a bit of a dark character indeed. I think this was as much a warning to me as it was for her. It was going to be difficult conveying that message which further unveiled that if she had the chance she should leave him and the job pronto! I am not a fortune-teller and this was particularly delicate advice to give.

I tend now to avoid domestic relationships with situations like these if I can.

There really was genuine concern from her mother coming through – basically conveying to me that she should get out now and move. I put those words in a discreet way to her but she knew what I was trying to say and her sudden facial expressions said it all about her current situation and life. This wasn't purely empathy on my side; I was feeling it and receiving validated information by Lana herself.

I was told it was her birthday this week, which she confirmed and I unusually but specifically felt the urge to immediately go out and buy her a little souvenir from the Catholic shop near the old church across the way. Lana was surprised to see me hand her this image of the Virgin Mary on a little gold background and responded by saying clearly but in a gentle way that; "I thought people like *you* don't believe in Christianity".

I smiled and said "well now you know – but whatever I think doesn't matter –this is a gift from your mother". Her mother had passed away of course and the fact that I had actually spent some of my own hard earned cash on a gift for a relative stranger, claiming and feeling the idea to be from her mother must have raised eyebrows with her husband again. This was on the assumption that she did repeat the salient points of my communications with her over those several days.

Some of you may think this is hilarious or even outrageous as our assumption is that the 'deceased' are buried six feet under and that's the end of it. Now here I was, handing over a little portrait of the Virgin Mary as gesture of symbolic significance, which was all due to an extraordinary spiritual experience and communication from the other side. Well, I have heard the saying pay it forward instead of paying back and perhaps that is what I did.

The following day I made my journey to do what would be my last reading for Lana. I was beginning to feel the spiritual link and vibrations becoming weaker. It's not that I didn't try, I tried so hard to – re-connect but it certainly wasn't like a telephone. In my experience, they come when they want to and not when we call them.

Unfortunately, unbeknown to me this time Lana's husband was waiting for me and he seemed to be extremely agitated by my presence. He was also chain-smoking at the top of the steep stairs, which was facing the elevated, wooden reception desk but with his back-turned and looking towards and through the antiquated windowpanes. I thought he hadn't seen me come up the stairs to the reception desk from behind him yet but I was wrong –he had actually been watching and scrutinising me approach the hotel through the upstairs window which he subsequently made clear in a threatening tonation.

As I cautiously greeted Lana at the front desk and began to complete my reading from the other side, I was suddenly disturbed by the strained voice of her husband who had most likely been smoking for decades. I tried to compose myself and was almost ready to do a continued reading for her but for some reason the 'link' seemed weak and I felt energy depletion. The buzz wasn't there as it should be. As I greeted Lana, her husband with intended and almost neurotic intrusion broke into my conversation with her as he inhaled once more from his rapidly depleting cigarette end.

It was as if someone had poked me in the back physically. He cleared his throat and asked me abruptly, "who the hell are you?" emphatically in a chest-beating, bellicose manner that it was his wife to whom I had been speaking to and that he had known her for over thirty years.

Ok, I thought, am I now facing a nutter or an incensed husband who thinks I am having an affair? This was laughable considering her maturity in years compared with mine and the real reasons for me being there at all as a hotel guest. So of course that was totally ruled out. I was now standing in front of his wife who was now slightly cowering behind the reception desk as she browsed in a distractive way through the accounts and guest book. She did indeed look uncomfortable.

His nicotine-stained fingers were now shaking either with simmering rage, bad nerves or a combination of both. He made it clear in an unconvincing way that he believed none of the spiritual details or explanations that I had given his wife over the last ten days or so. Quite simply, he told me to make myself disappear soon or he would do it! He really did believe I was some kind of spy and he was uncomfortable with me communicating with his wife –or so it seems, that is one interpretation of it.

By now I was feeling his insecurities as well as his hostility towards me and as if he had something truly to hide. I needed to find a way out, literally a sharp exit.

Through this event with Lana and my readings for her, I soon learnt a lesson pretty quickly. I never saw Lana working at that hotel again. Did she take her mother's advice or did her husband do something and take her away or even something more sinister? Was her husband really part of some gambling gang as he had also implied to me?

What I do now is that the experience became my very own personal and profound spiritual awakening, which changed not only Lana but also me. I finally received all the proof I needed and knew I wanted to do something with it for a good purpose in the future. I still keep those written notes with me of that spectacular and moving experience. I often carry them as a souvenir and testimony whenever I return to Singapore and I walk past that little hotel. This is not just to reminisce, but is a constant reminder that it really did happen. When in times of doubt and periods of a confidence booster I just look at those notes written and inspired from the heavens.

Chapter 4

A Little Classroom Entertainment

Whilst returning and visiting an international college in Asia that I had once previously worked in, I was asked to offer some input to a former colleague's class of about 40 students or more. This was in my very earliest days of 'awakenings' for which I still hadn't yet realised the potential of what was to come later in my teaching career. Here I was now, as a guest and visitor rather than an employee being invited by a good Burmese teaching colleague and friend, Kyaw Aung. His parents I later met personally and include in my chapter on Burma for which we experienced another unusual event.

Since I wasn't officially teaching there now, I decided to do something a little more adventurous, communicative and creative for the lesson. I was up for it, felt in a good mood and was feeling a familiar buzz of psychic energy. What did I have to lose? They can't fire me – I don't work there. Ha! I suddenly felt full of vitality and relished the chance of being in front of a class again after a six-month absence from teaching whilst travelling in the region.

My friend Kyaw, in Burmese, pronounced 'Jaw' said, "Jonny, it's all yours –I need to relax a bit after all the marking and teaching load this semester so keep them happy this afternoon but I will be here on hand to help it along if needed". He sat alongside me happily observing and coaxing the class.

He didn't leave the classroom but he did want a much-deserved break and continued to observe and seemed happy enough for me to choose the topic of the day. There are cases when teachers prefer to team teach too and this seemed like a good idea – however, I wouldn't recommend my approach that followed!

This was the last afternoon period and some stimulating activity of an entertaining nature is what they needed after a tedious or laborious day of studying, when students tend to be their most lethargic. I know this to be true as some of the students are expected to digest six hours or more of English a day, so I have empathy. Many go to sleep extremely late and get up early for school or college and arrive half-awake because of it.

Everyone talks about ghosts, spirits, and other spiritual phenomena at some stage in their lives. Just think of all those schools that introduce Halloween as a topic and festive activity from Kindergarten age onwards. In some parts of Asia they also have the hungry ghost festival too, which adds momentum to the topic. It felt as good a time as ever to discuss it as a topic but without intentionally 'scaring the pants off' them as the English idiom goes.

Here was my chance, propped up on a small raised platform; I got up eagerly with coloured, marking pens to the whiteboard in my clean white, pressed shirt, black slacks and shiny new shoes which I could see my face in. With an eager zest, writing the word in large, bold letters, 'Spirits' on the extra-long whiteboard, I asked the multi-national class if anyone could brainstorm ideas related to that particular word. Mostly made up of Chinese, Thai, Vietnamese, a few Cambodians, Burmese and Mongolian, there were also a couple of European and Scandinavian students who were present. The class was almost immediately attentive though not necessarily as easy to convince, but I think most westerners tend to be like that.

Sure enough, it led into the spirits subject, not of whisky and vodka – a popular and ubiquitous, alcoholic beverage in Thailand but of ghosts, sixth-sense, psychic, haunted and so on – even the word 'Caspar' from the famous movie was brainstormed.

As you can imagine, the majority of South Asian students within the class were more often than not superstitious, so that also helped the communication process and did not hinder it for the most part. Not that superstition is the main key to opening the 'psychic door' but I have found that it opens the mind for those conditions to allow it to work more successfully and in a more fluid way. And of course, then there are the existing energies of the students, the family spirits that they bring along with them and the willingness to be open. It all contributes.

Standing at the front of the class I felt a spiritual buzz with an energetic pull to the right, and by now I was already feeling the adrenalin. Maybe it was more than just adrenalin but it felt like something was actually going to happen. I placed my outstretched hand into the air and asked the students to the right of the class in a group of three, which one of the Asian females had the connection to Hong Kong. No response. I eagerly pursued this and said again to the class, 'I won't let this go as I am sure it is one of the two girls sitting next to each other'.

By now, all the students were sitting upright and alert. One of the Thai students now got up discreetly but enthusiastically to draw the blinds for some reason, maybe to add a bit of mystical atmosphere to the occasion. Of course I had a few puzzled looks but one of the older girls (all young adults) finally held up her hand and blurted out that her sister was living in Hong Kong although she was not originally from there.

Yes, who is the oddball, a teacher confusing a class with odd questions and his hand held out, I hear you say? Well it wasn't my own class of students anyway. You may say by now, what's the point of all this? However, at the time I had picked up a vibrational buzz – psychic adrenalin to be more precise, and not knowing what to do with using this dispensable energy, I introduced a piece of theatrical entertainment for a class of forty intrigued 19 to 25-year-old students. Theatrics is also something, which I feel adds to the atmosphere when teaching.

Of course the outstretched hand wasn't always necessary and perhaps a little intimidating. However, this was just similar to the experience where your maths teacher was pointing to you personally and asking for an immediate response to a mathematical question to jog your memory. I confidently asked the boy at the back, second on the right to confirm for me that he knew the story of *the* ghost or spirit that was seen and *known* about within his family.

With what felt like psychic Adrenalin and with full radar of that 'knowing' feeling for me again, there was no doubt to say what felt right. It couldn't have been a chance guessing as how many of us have a story of the family ghost or spirit walking around our home? Not so many, I believe. Well, not everybody that is.

There was no response to my question of the personal family ghost as he reluctantly shook his head. I said, "I can't let this go; I know it *IS* you and I know that this event is in your family". Please think and confirm for me again. The class went quiet as heads swiftly moved his way. The spotlight was on him but it was also on me if I had been incorrect. There was a reluctant nod and the boy finally admitted that the spirit of his grandmother had been seen and heard around the house but not told to anyone else outside the family for one reason or another.

This was his chance I thought and I asked for a round of applause for the boy to come to the front and tell the whole class in English about his story. Not one student asked to leave the class which by now seemed to be gripped with excited curiosity and alertness. This followed a myriad of questions from the now intrepid and enthusiastic class whilst I added the newly acquired vocabulary on the whiteboard, which mostly was elicited and encouraged from them.

However, as always there is usually at least one skeptic to upset the process, given the chance. One Chinese student in a deep voice with arms ostentatiously folded and chest protruding like a proud pigeon said firmly and loudly in slightly, broken English –"I don't believe!"

"Ahh," I said to the class. "Leon Tan Ho doesn't believe it. But, by the end of the lesson, I know he will change his mind!" I quickly responded.

What had I said? God forbid. What made me say and blindly reassure the class of that statement with such confidence? It is this 'knowing' that encourages us to say what we wouldn't otherwise have felt the need to say. We may call it the sixth sense or intuition. I was of course, taking a gamble with my feelings and with this student still with hands folded across his chest in a resolute, skeptical and defensive manner. I went on to confirm with him that he was expecting to have gone to a European country to study but that it hadn't worked out and that his relatives were already over there. Neither did I know why I said it or thought about where the information may be coming from. It just felt significant enough to take the risk and it felt 'right' just at that moment.

Meanwhile, I carefully wrote in big letters with a blue whiteboard marker the word, *FRANCE* on the front of my hand with my back turned to the class and hand closed but with inquisitive looks. Half the class was already engrossed in asking the other boy to confirm the information about the spirit of his grandmother who by now had already pulled the blinds to make it more conducive to a séance! Now that did take me by surprise, despite me not giving permission, I didn't want to cut the flow of information, which could affect my concentration. But after all, this was entertainment too. Just before the end of the class I asked the skeptical student, *Leon Tan Ho* to stand up in front of the class, turn around and confirm the correct country that he had planned to study in but that had not been able to.

My heart was jumping as I knew my reputation, as well as confidence would be on the line even though I was not officially working here any longer, in a public auditorium on platform or under any obligation to prove anything. For me it was a personal test which, to be honest, was spontaneous. It was all done with the spring of an energetic, eager opportunist for which I had and still do have an avid enthusiasm of the supernatural, or *'The other side'* as some of us term the afterlife.

Oh, and that student, Leon Tan Ho. It still mattered to me and yes, if the truth is known I was initially irritated by him, which ironically made it more of a challenge, a test or an extreme embarrassment if I got it wrong. Statistically everything should have been on a scale more towards the low chance percentage anyway. I don't particularly like tests and am sure spirit doesn't either. If someone asks you to prove yourself at the snap of a finger would you do it? And for that matter why should you? If ignorance is indelibly part of one's beliefs, doctrine and personality then it may be like trying to get blood out of a stone – those types of demanding people do exist.

Finally, Leon Tan stood up proudly and told the class the country he was supposed to have gone to. Chest puffed out, he said quite confidently, proudly and in a rather gleeful manner 'FRANCE'. I asked him to repeat the country 'France' for all to hear. My heart was now beginning to beat a little faster with the hint of a satisfied smile. He spelt it alphabetically and pronounced it phonetically even louder a second time "F-R-A-N-C-E – FRANCE!"

I thought to myself, yes, ok, they get the message and so do I. I immediately held up my hand to the class, moved and displayed in panoramic fashion so that everyone could see and said jubilantly, 'Thank you very much, please now look at the word in blue ink written on my hand'. The blue bold letters spelling the word 'FRANCE' resulted in an immediate round of applause for me and a great end to the day. I was now in an ebullient mood and thanked god and my spirit guide even if I wasn't aware of a real guide at that period in my life or fully aware how it all happened – but it was all well worth it.

That class went back to their dorms happily and no doubt had a few discussions about it to their own teacher and friends later. It wasn't until much later that I knew I was now experiencing something different. It confirmed for me that this ability that I had put on hold, in an unconscious delay for at least ten years previously to teaching, was already making significant waves into my life. It was just that I hadn't noticed it so much and certainly hadn't believed in myself enough to demonstrate it as a communication tool for whatever situation, form or shape that should be or would ensue later on in life.

Think of how many of us doubt ourselves at all kinds of skills, abilities or even sports but then push ourselves later to say 'gosh, I did that? I really didn't think I could'. Or worse still, those that never encouraged you or laughed at your hidden talents therefore stifling any progress that could change your life for the better. It happens on a daily basis. There are those people who refuse to accept anything other than what they are quite comfortable to want to understand. Anything outside their understanding of the world as they have been led to believe has to be rejected. However, in this situation it is true that it is easier to have been more doubtful, as we are not dealing with the tangible and physically obvious. That's a disadvantage of this phenomenon, which perhaps makes it more intriguing and inhibiting publicly.

That classroom entertainment episode leaves me with an original and lengthy e-mail report that I had written and sent to my good Thai friend, Zack in Thailand. It concerned another psychic event rather than what I had assumed at the time to be clairvoyant and spiritual. However, often they can be both intertwined as one feeds into the other. It's virtually in diary format as recorded on the day and I felt it worthy of taking a page out of an average eventful day in the classroom to share it here.

From: jonny@
To: Zack@
SUBJECT: Friday Afternoon class
Time: 01:01:57

Hi Zack
How are you? Did you get my urgent text message?
I wanted to mention about another of my spiritual experiences today.
This afternoon was a strange one with a mixed bag of energies.
I totally lost track that it was Friday afternoon as though I was in some kind of trance for a brief moment. Coming to the end of the day I was also tired.
I scolded three 'gangster' boys for disturbing the class and told them to leave, which they did so in a red-hot flustered manner.
I raised my voice in annoyance. Immediately they left the class, I decided to explain to the rest of the students that I was not normally an angry person. (As I am well aware in Asia they look down on those who lose their cool.) But, that they had to understand that we cannot let three idle and obstreperous students destroy the peace and harmony of the entire class.
Well, I guess that is where my spirit guide jumped in right there at that moment seeing I was having a hard time.
Those annoying students who I had reprimanded and told to stand outside the class never came back for the rest of the period and possibly on Monday, I am not their friend anymore.
I was actually glad they didn't return.
That left me with a sudden surge of emotional *and vibrant energy* so I decided right there and then to do a bit of 'magic' for the rest of the class. I called it 'magic' so that they will accept it and understand it better.

On a gut feeling or hunch I wrote on the white-board 'Sixth Sense'.

I held my hand out and above the students facing me. In each specific part of the room that I said was such an activity, animal, pet, and car, in their home or life, whatever – each consecutive reading was correct including the specific colour. Total seven in a row!

I started by asking a mature, cheerful Mongolian student to draw an object and a named colour in big letters on plain paper. She was quite enthusiastic and obliging to do this. I turned my back to the white-board just like we did in groups at Psychic college training in London, and then kindly asked the willing and enthusiastic student to step forward and place the paper in my hand behind my back – I was blindfolded.

I immediately saw in my mind's eye the colour 'WHITE' and a large lake written and drawn in Pencil before she had actually shown me the paper. I drew the lake and wrote the word 'white' on the white board then turned to confirm it. It had indeed been scribbled in pencil and was indeed showing the shape of a lake!

I got a round of applause. It certainly felt like total sixth sense or spiritual help coming to me at the right time and that 'buzz' of energy again.

It went on as I had described the family car as a silver Japanese pick-up with a blue-stripe 'just recently purchased by one of the student's father' with other meticulous details such as the model, and the student who lived next to an enchanting, but deep turquoise lake with long reeds on the perimeter, which I had just drawn on the whiteboard. I was on a roll today!

Then there was the Vietnamese student at the back of the class with the white pet rabbit who I specifically chose and confirmed the information. This was followed by describing the image of a skinny, long legged, mid-brown and white dog with a sunken stomach belonging to a Burmese student at the front of the class in the third seat to the left and just knowing which seat he was in too.

Zack, I had described it in graphic detail using my hands and body so it was clear enough.

You know I wouldn't tell you rubbish.

I remember on this occasion that I was able to sense and select the specific area of the class the students were sitting in so it was not guessing by so called law of averages. I felt I was being guided.

So, all in all, a productive afternoon, even if I was highly charged from an earlier commotion due to some disruptive students who I had ejected from the class. This was all being observed by a new Canadian teacher called Tanya who had just popped in for the afternoon on a trial. She seemed to be oblivious to what I was really doing which was amusing.

I think she thought I had made it up or that is was some kind of fun lesson plan from an English Language game in a resource teaching worksheet –hilarious, of course.

Surprisingly, one of the Indonesian students shouted out "'David Copperfield!' teacher!" to which I swiftly responded that David Copperfield is an illusionist, explaining that I am not, but thanked her kindly.

After, I reflected on the eventful afternoon and excitedly forwarded an enthusiastic text message on my mobile phone to my brother back in the UK to also let him know.

Whilst I had to pinch myself that it really was true, it was all shared in harmless fun and enjoyment by the whole class at the end of the week on the Friday.

Let me know what you think.

Jonny

Chapter 5

Marco's Communication: Dream or premonition?

There were other things happening. More prolific now, these experiences began to manifest in a variety of ways with different forms of communication, whether as a message or as what we sometimes call a 'sixth sense hunch'. Occasionally, paranormal activity such as garden lights came on by themselves at night without being linked to the electricity and flashing towards my window as I worked on my computer. I knew something wanted me to go out to the garden and take more photos and some of that material can be seen in this book but mostly can be seen via my website.

But it starts way back in the schoolyard, and one other significant clairvoyance experience will remain with me forever. I still clearly remember as if it was only yesterday, having to watch a shocking documentary on road accidents for road safety awareness in school, as a teenager and myself a pupil, and one year before final grade. This public information movie was for several classes together and we were all sat close to each other with the rest of the students behind in rows on raised levels in order to view the large screen better. It was very graphic and gory but was part of the road safety awareness scheme for schools at that time. There were moments I and other students had to avert our eyes.

One boy from my class called Marco, who I had known since early primary school had sat directly behind me with his good friend, Dean. Amongst many, in one scene there was a graphic movie clip of a fatal, road crash scene. It was a motorbike rider and passengers. I remember quite clearly, and swiftly turning round to Marco with an ominous look, staring right into his eyes and pausing. He responded with an irritated and uneasy "what's wrong?" as he contorted his eyebrows and squishing his nose. I responded with an uncomfortable and perhaps unconvincing, "uh, nothing" and slowly turned back to the screen self-consciously embarrassed at the synchronicity of the timely gaze. I was not accustomed to doing that. I looked back at his face, eye to eye again. I wasn't exactly sure what I was feeling but it was unusual, something unpleasant and elusive.

In the weeks that followed the whole class went up to the mountains for a school adventure trip on what some may call a summer camp – except this was mid-spring season. For a few of those nights we also stayed at an old Manor house on the top of a steep, rugged hill overlooking a breathtaking drop, which was covered in bracken. In the distance, the terrain was dotted with rugged Welsh Ponies which one local farmer once told me were as 'hard as nails'. They were feeding on the thick hill grass next to gently flowing streams trickling through the uneven green turf and landscape. It was just us and a few grazing animals in the wilderness of a small mountain in Wales with notorious, unpredictable weather.

We eventually camped on the top of the Welsh mountains of the Snowdonia National Park for the rest of the endurance. All of this was and still is covered in bracken and gorse-clad landscape dotted with sharply rising, craggy cliffs of indigenous Welsh slate. Wild buzzards circled above us in the distance.

It was almost the end of April and the smell of spring was still fresh in the air but the snow was still at the top. It was so chilly up there and we all hit an unexpected and frightening blizzard coming back but fortunately, somehow managing to find our way down the mountain as a group intact through thick mist. We found our way using just a compass and by order of the sole teacher in the group, we all held onto each other's shoulders in caterpillar-file because the visibility was so restricted. The only comfort was hard mint sweets being offered, but we were all so nervous we hardly said a word until we made it safely to the bottom. Some of us could have certainly got lost and even perished that day as we attempted to descend the mountain. Understandably, there is an indelible memory of that school adventure which remains intact and vivid in my mind.

I shared a tent with Marco and his best friend, Dean. The only locals were the rugged, mountain ponies and weather-hardy hill Sheep. At that time, Dean was in the other tent across the slope but would come in to chat with his best friend, Marco since they were always together at school. I remember both of us watching some strange lights in the sky before we slept in the chilly, damp tent and discussing whether they were UFOs or not. Those lights certainly looked unusual as we fixed our concentration on them. I had been an ardent UFO enthusiast from the age of ten and had witnessed a few of the officially, unexplainable occurrences which had also been reported by sound witnesses in newspapers later on. After leaving school, I had been interviewed by reporters for a local newspaper and had one or two stories printed. I am sure they weren't aware I was only a teenager when being interviewed on the telephone!

'*Local UFO group reports aliens in the area*' was the heading – or something to that affect. How embarrassing it was when my mother's friend asked her if her son had been in the local newspaper concerning UFO's and aliens.

Later, during the blackness of night in the cold mountain air, Marco suddenly shouted out in his sleep "Dean, Dean!!" He tossed and turned in the rather cramp conditions in our compact tent. Suddenly and abruptly with an apparent knee-jerk reaction he awoke and sat up rigid as if in a nightmare. It was if a corpse had suddenly sat up out of a coffin mysteriously with a gasp of air similar to a jack-in-the-box. His eyes were fixed through the flapping slit of the tent vent from the blustery, outside mountain wind. He was now looking into space as if he had seen or experienced something terrible and for a few moments he seemed oblivious to my presence. I just sat there quietly in suspense watching his frozen and startled stare from the moonlight shadow, which permeated the tent canvas highlighting his silhouette.

In our drafty, cold tent on top of the mountain with the school group, the night-air was certainly cold and windy out there. Just for a short while, I anxiously fixed my gaze on him in the darkness, sitting upright as he mumbled something from the disturbed, bad dream. He was breathing heavily as if he had been panting in a race to get away from something or someone.

Less than one month following that mountain trip event we received a telephone call saying that Marco had just been killed in a motorbike accident after leaving a sharp bend and hitting a concrete wall. He was pronounced dead on arrival and 'in bad shape' according to the doctors in the emergency ward at that time. He had only just reached 16 years of age.

He had been with his close friend Dean, who was on his own motorbike at the time but had remained a witness to it, was unscathed and who later that very day in shock, came to my home to inform me personally. One week prior to the accident, Marco had told me he would be 'coming to take me up the mountain on the bike and would see me on Saturday' with Dean. He never made it.

As I try to piece the signs together, I truly believe that they were related to the eventual fatal accident. I am also convinced he had dreamt of his oncoming early death. I am in no doubt that I can link the unusual experience during the road safety film viewing in school where I had faced Marco ominously and sensing unconsciously what was to come. If I only had a time machine, but time stood still then and I remember this as if it was today. It's a strange thing 'time' but then we have all at least heard of and experienced the déjà-vu feeling even if we don't accept premonitions.

A short while later after his death I met Marco in a vivid dream. Of course, he was not in the physical state he would have been at the time of the tragic motorbike accident at all. He was wearing what appeared to be a white suit and was now guiding me back through the school. I recall asking him "how can this be? You are dead Marco".

He just laughed and said – "I know" with his usual characteristic and sprightly chuckle.

He had always been lively in character and humour and this was reflected in which he came back to me in another dream about two years later. This time, he was showing me coffins in what seemed to be a mortuary. We were playing in, running around and taking a look inside other empty coffins, playing 'hide and seek'.

More recently, I paid a visit to a famous Spiritualist church in London where at one time the famous, former Successful medium Doris Stokes would do platform readings. Sitting here in the audience, we were now being given a demonstration by a European psychic artist who drew portraits of spirit.

I thought it would be interesting to see other people's facial reactions to the artist's material and stayed on a little longer. There was a sign on the wall mentioning that we should not leave during a performance, which is understandable as we don't want to break the concentration of the medium's link with the other side. To my surprise the psychic artist almost immediately began to draw on her wide, flip chart of large portrait-sized paper so we could all get a clear enough view of her work in action.

Directing her hand towards my direction down the aisle and identifying me as the link, she explained in detail that she had a young male with her who had been in a motorcycle accident.

I promptly confirmed to her the rest of the detailed information that he had indeed died in a motorcycle accident – on a bend in a rural area by a bridge. That was exactly what and where it happened. She went on to remind me that he is around me often. Of course, I knew who it was as soon she pointed towards me with her arm outstretched to identify and confirm that I was familiar to his spirit even though my heart was beating a little faster knowing it had to be Marco. I was anticipating what he might say.

She had now completed the drawing of his portrait, which showed his image just at the age he left this world including his hairstyle, distinct eyes and jacket he had on that day! I was touched and felt grateful to know he still acknowledged me as I did him, despite us not being close buddies – but he was a good classmate and I had known him right through from primary to senior school. I still keep that psychic portrait of him rolled up in my storage cupboard.

A strange occurrence followed. A few days later I returned to the same Spiritualist church in London but with a different medium on the platform who described Marco's presence again. This time the medium announced he had a message for me. 'You have to watch what you are saying to people'. I knew what that meant. It related to psychic readings and he knew about that too.

I know his death was a horrific shock for all his family. I also will never forget the day the teacher came into the class to ask us to all stand and say prayers for Marco's sister. She had passed over at the tender age of just six years old from a rare medical condition only seven years previously, before he had later lost his own life.

I will never forget his little sister's bright, wide eyes as we stared at each other through the railings a month or so before her death. We were communicating in some sort of way despite hardly speaking a word to each other as she swung from the playground railings not taking our eyes off each other with curiosity. I was only eight years old myself at the time but I see her there now, wearing a little patterned, autumn coat with fluffy hood as she was twirling over the railings that separated us.

She had just started primary school but how photographic of our memory bank to deftly retain such poignant moments. What is it that freezes time in the form of a photographic memory? Perhaps it is that unconscious 'knowing' again, the sensing of someone soon to be removed from this life. Maybe that is why we remember a simple, yet otherwise ordinary face-to-face experience more lucidly and profoundly, which haunts us for the rest of our lives.

The spirits have now passed over to the other side but the memories and images still stick with us as we remember them and specific moments in time – especially if it was the last moment we ever saw them here in the physical dimension. I often wonder too if those that passed away so young were reborn quite quickly and sometimes into the same family – but that is just a thought to ponder. Then again, would they want *us* to forget them? I think not.

There is the benefit of those in sprit informing and consoling us that they have not disappeared into thin air. Letting us know they are free from pain and suffering and not to grieve over them would make sense for a reason to communicate. We often hear in spiritualism that our feelings and strong thoughts of emotion attract them so we have to be aware of this.

For those of us who do believe in mediumship and spiritual contact from the other side, I believe spirit also has to be given the chance to try and make contact with their loved ones. There is a place for god, as we perceive it and a place for our loved ones who are in my opinion are active in the other dimension in spirit too. This is not often welcomed or wanted for most of the bereaved, due to a range of inhibited beliefs.

'RIP' – *Rest in Peace* on a headstone is universal but I am sure they are more often *restless* with their feelings and emotional attachments firmly still linked to the physical, at least for a while. However, belief or not, spirit will try to make contact in ways that would be appropriate to the bereaved when they can. This could be in dreams or feelings of their presence and the sensitivity to spirit around us. For example, when you pick up a photograph of the deceased, your thoughts and emotions can be relayed to them. It may not even be a photograph that triggers the feeling of their presence and attraction to your own thoughts and emotions. I have heard of many who saw a feather appear on several occasions where there were no sign of any white birds or indeed, any birds at all in their home and where there was no existence of feathered pillows etc.

Some may say this is not spiritual phenomenon and that I understand, but when sights, sounds and fragrances become stronger around you which relate to your deceased family or friends then there has to be something more happening here. But feathers mysteriously appearing in the home are to some seen as a sign from the heavens.

I was so aware that whilst teaching, many students were being watched by some of their close relatives in spirit. I do not believe that all of my experiences and evidence about their lives were simply and only psychic alone. It was just too strong at times, especially when on occasions I was receiving images of a student's deceased relative wearing the clothes they wore just before they had died. Some would say this could be disconcerting in a classroom environment; however these visions were never presented to me as spooky – it was just as if they were fit and healthy in the physical. It was quite the contrary, and most of the time I felt the warmth of compassion emanating from the spirit and particularly towards their young relative sitting in the classroom or wherever.

Practicing psychics and mediums have been around for a very long time. If only we could more often successfully access and listen to the spirit within, including our hunches and intuition in our busy lives. It may lead us to a more positive communication to relieve the hazards of everyday life. With spirit contact however, this communication of course, depends on factors such as the receptiveness of the reader/communicator, but also whether the spirit of those passed over is available or wants to come through. This in my view doesn't mean that there is an 'away' sign on their spiritual door – just that it may not be their time to make contact.

Repeatedly we hear that mediums admit that they can't contact whoever the sitter/client wishes to communicate with in spirit. Many agree that it is potluck who comes through and the medium can only give what information they get on the day from a spirit related to the sitter at random. This is also my experience too. It's not like a direct telephone call to the other side from exactly who and when we want to hear, in my opinion.

Dreams of premonition

I am aware through gradual experience of course, that spirits come to us in different ways. As with Marco's death there was some pre-feeling and it was not the only shock to the system to come. However, these experiences or visions can only be as good as the receptive, mental faculties we have that may or may not be finely-tuned enough at the time. For some of us, this may occur when you are asleep and this is what I discuss next concerning another motoring accident related to me.

Several years ago I awoke up in a pool of sweat in what seemed a lengthy dream and a most horrible one. I clearly recall the final moments of it. Towards the end of the dream for which I remember most vividly, I was being ushered into a hospital ward. As I turned the corner into the emergency ward in my dream, I was sickened to suddenly see my mother with her hands bandaged, stone-faced with an intravenous drip in her arm and face covered with a mask of some sort. My father was saying something at floor-level on a hospital trolley bed. I was so shocked by this dream that I thought it was just a horrible nightmare. The feelings within the dream were that of trauma and shock but I put it to one side, as just being some kind of nightmare.

About three weeks later I was waiting for a ride to be picked up at the bus terminal by my parents, which would have been just after office hours. I waited for well over an hour and a half and then another further half an hour as I paced up and down the bus terminal. This was too long so something was wrong, I felt. My father was usually very reliable but this didn't seem right. I decided to leave and head for the train station and make my own way back home, a thirty-mile or so journey. Since neither of my parents had a mobile phone on them at the time I hadn't used mine nor switched it on that day to save battery power. Besides, they wouldn't be at home as my mother was also being collected from the office at her work from another town many miles away. I assumed they were on their way through the narrow country lanes to eventually collect me but delayed for one reason or another.

However, whilst on the train I had the urge to suddenly switch it on as it had been off for a while to save the dwindling battery power. To my surprise it rang immediately as I switched it on. It was an urgent call from the hospital. My parents had just been in a serious car accident and were now in the hospital emergency ward. They had hit a snow-gritting truck in a narrow country lane coming in the opposite direction on a bend and hit it head on. They had to be cut from the vehicle by the fire emergency services.

The staff nurse on the phone asked where I was at that moment. Naturally, I told them I was on the train on my way home. I was told to get off at the next station and the police would be waiting to take me to the local County Hospital. I was chauffeured off by the waiting two policemen in the patrol car only to be told, on arrival at the hospital to stay in the car until they came back from the reception.

As I waited briefly with anticipation and concern I was then given the 'Ok, you can go in now.' As I followed one of the senior ward staff on duty down the corridor I immediately began to feel a déjà-vu and it was getting more vibrant as I approached the ward where my parents were in the emergency room. I felt I was walking through a slow motion film. This *was* my dream.

As I turned the corner of the ward there was my mother in a bed with her hands held in the air for support to relieve bone fractures and a facemask for oxygen with a tube in her arm. I winced, reluctant to show my emotion as my father lay on the hospital trolley-bed on floor level. It was my mother who bore the brunt of the crash as her ribs were broken in several places and her spleen was punctured, so was left in Hospital for a further two weeks or more. All she could muster was a restricted, forced-grimace of a painful smile and groan. Her hands were ice-cold.

This was one of the significant, true stories from my diary that I really found hard to write or feel comfortable with here for obvious reasons, but I have put it down on paper and recorded it as I felt it certainly valid and worthy enough as a poignant and very real premonition. It would be nice to know that we could have positive premonitions rather than negative ones. However, there have been accounts about people who have had premonitions, which saved lives.

These involved reports of people who, at the last moment decided not to get on a plane, trains and other forms of transport which later ended in tragedy. Scouring through the history books, the Titanic had far less passengers than had original booked cabins. It was also known that a significant number of the workers on the ship didn't arrive for duty on that fateful journey. In my case however, could I have changed the events? Had it not been enough to realise the difference between just a dream, nightmare and a prediction as a warning, is debatable.

If we could switch on sixth sense clairvoyance at will, like a light bulb then we wouldn't have half the disasters that occur in this world. If only we could unlock the code and that's the billion-dollar question. It is my belief that sometimes our own super sixth sense informs us and at other times it is being relayed from spirit. This is certainly another dimension of the spiritual spectrum that I began to experience on my travels, and particularly, though not exclusively, around The Far East where I spent some considerable time.

Chapter 6

The Vietnam connection

It was during a return trip to Vietnam that I was virtually pulled out of bed by what felt like one attention seeking spirit as I rested in a three storey-tall, back street home. I had had dreams and experiences of spiritual activity in the past but this was different. I had made over four trips back to Vietnam including Hanoi, Hoi an, Danang and Ho Chi Minh city – the latter being formerly known as Saigon. This time I was mostly here on invitation from my former students and their families who welcomed me. I had previously taught them in Singapore and was cordially greeted by them on arrival.

I found them to be most hospitable to me. I have fond memories from some of the positive and productive, spontaneous readings I had been able to do there for a selected few. I really did enjoy the ambience of the whole trip including the friendship I encountered in my experiences. It may certainly be a different experience for other visitors to Vietnam, and there are dangers, but this had been my situation. And yes, I could have been an ordinary tourist browsing the plethora of shops tucked away in backstreets searching for local artwork, traditional lacquer ware, woodcarvings or even silverware – but I didn't have the space in my luggage anyway. I don't travel like that. I had already generously been given a few gifts from my host families including a hand-made silk-tie and an ornamental, golden passenger – tricycle, which once prolifically represented the traditional form of transport.

I am aware that Vietnamese are mostly superstitious regarding the spiritual, which is traditionally and culturally, similar to Thailand as nearly every home has a spirit house nestled in some corner of the home or office. China in my view has been an influence with the worship of their ancestors, which plays a big part in Vietnam. More recently in history, If we consider the tragedies that the Vietnamese endured in recent decades it is no wonder it has a need for psychics which are still being used to locate the bodies of their missing soldiers. It has been said that around 400,000 people are still missing.

Whilst sitting outside a coffee shop on the banks of a river I said to Than Tran, one of my former English Language students, that it was funny because I could sense a soldier's spirit around him. I wasn't trying to do this. It just happened as we were beginning to drink our coffee. I knew this because of the dowdy-coloured military uniform I was sensing. However, following this image, the word 'engagement' was simultaneously being clearly expressed.

He quickly took notice of this as his eyes lit up and went on to explain that his father had just been to look for his brother's remains in a field and was led to his body by a top government psychic. He lost his brother in the Vietnam War. These psychics are often hired by the government to search for the remains of their loved ones who died in the war. It is believed by the psychic that the spirit of the soldier leads them to the remains and it is my personal belief that this is pure mediumship as there is active spirit intelligence involved giving directions to specific locations. Of course there are positive results too.

In Vietnam, even at the present time of writing, most families still need closure and this is one other method of doing so by hiring a reputable psychic. My former student, Than Tran went on to say his brother had actually just got engaged in Danang, therefore verifying the engagement ring I was sensing. I was happy for him, as for so long I hadn't been able to prove or pick up anything from sixth sense or spirit for this particular, amiable and affable Vietnamese friend up to that date.

It also intrigues me to think that the spirit of the family follows their relatives around. If not, then are certainly able to be aware where they are at any time and what they are doing. This of course is on the assumption that the spirit has not yet passed on to an even higher dimension or even another incarnation, depending on one's belief. Of course there is also fact, and for that I simply cannot prove, as I am not on the *other side* yet.

Meanwhile, whilst in Saigon, I had a vivid dream of myself walking outside in the backstreet area of District 1, in Ho Chi Min City (Saigon). At this time I was staying as an invite with the parents of one of my Vietnamese hosts on the top floor in a shady backstreet area. This home had fortified gates, which seem to be common in parts of Asia and ominously laced with deliberately broken glass inserted along the perimeters of the gates and walls. The strongest and largest padlocks I have ever seen were firmly attached to the steel gates as an extra deterrent. I felt like a caged animal.

Most of the wealthier owned Vietnamese houses or buildings seem to be at least three floors tall and built in narrow box fashion – at least that's my opinion of course, and if the owner has money they are built that way if they can afford it depending on space. They are often well fortified with high steel gates for obvious reasons.

Meanwhile, in this dream, I found myself walking directly past the house I was currently staying at. I was suddenly aimed at what seemed to be a large stone, which fortunately seemed to erratically bounce off the pavement around me, rocked the ground and then shook me hard. Simultaneously, it was like someone had grabbed me physically and jolted me mentally both at the same time. If you have had an electric shock then you will understand the feeling with a little more clarity.

I was being shaken quite vigorously but only for a few seconds and this time I felt considerable energy – the force of a mind and spirit. So much so, I literally fell out of the large comfortable double bed I was in and onto the cold marble floor – yes, I was by now hanging out the side! The experience was similar to someone shouting at you for attention with a loudspeaker whilst physically feeling their energy and not merely the audible voice. Think about it – how else would a spirit, and if it is spirit, attempt to communicate to get attention?

The jolt immediately woke me up but this time I didn't say to myself "oh what a 'bad' dream" and then go back to sleep. Not this time. I was abruptly woken up and, rubbing my eyes I said quite clearly "What? What do you want? Look, I know you want something but I am not Vietnamese and I need to get more information if you want me to get the message". Then I 'translated' it though my thoughts as we do.

With all the psychic angel card readings I was set out to do in subsequent days, as arranged with former students and their friends, I think it is not surprising that someone on the other side wanted to pass a message before I got to them. Unfortunately, in this particular case I will never know. I didn't manage to work out a message at 4am or if there even was one. I do not believe this was imagination prompted by a dream – definitely not. It was another awakening to spirit as part of the learning process and experience of communication, but I do feel the more one begins to notice the signs then the receptivity grows in a variety of spiritual and psychic dimensions.

The next day after informing my Vietnamese hosts about the attention seeking spirit, I was horrified to hear that a murder had taken place directly outside their house gates a year previously. I was glad that I hadn't gone down that alley late at night after hearing that. I try my best to avoid negative 'hot spots'. Since I was not in touch with any of the living relatives of that victim, I didn't feel I was able to or neither had the normal means to relay any further relevant information. There have been some occasions I have been able to pick up foreign names with unusual pronunciation from time to time. However, I do know of top mediums who are doing this and they travel far and wide relaying message and information from spirit in foreign languages. Sometimes these have been full names in their own language, which I on occasion have been able to spell out – phonetically at least.

I do sympathise with all those frustrated spirits who are trying to let their friends and family know that they are fine and not just turned into ashes. For example, can you imagine passing away at short notice in the middle of daily life when suddenly you snuff it leaving behind a myriad of unfinished business? Most will have left business undone and surely would like to amend or even somehow try to continue what they had left behind. I don't feel it would immediately be any different for a spirit in the after-life.

After all, their whole life in this world was all they ever knew up to that moment just before they passed away and therefore we shouldn't assume their memory banks or the emotional links have been erased. This is of course on the assumption that we accept life after death as sacrosanct, which naturally I vehemently believe, due to my own personal experience. Of course, this belief has been influenced and enhanced as a result of my varied spiritual communications.

Of course there are there are those academics who pontificate and say the consciousness does not survive the body when it dies but I am one of the many 'witnesses' to know this is nonsense. The proof is in the eating! I don't subscribe to the idea that the deceased just say, "ok well that's it then guys. Nice to have known you –good luck!" Yes, good luck, RIP! Rest in Peace? I will say the only things that rest are the bones and dust.

In dreams we can be mistaken for thinking that they were just exactly that – images of seeing friends or relatives we once knew who were alive. In the case I mentioned earlier, I would have been in the alpha-state. It has been said that the mind can be influenced in this phase of 'sleep' and I was certainly influenced enough to take action and be notified by a lively spirit who probably knew I was on my way to do a reading the same day or in the coming week. I can't prove that but that was my hunch.

Family quest

Ricky (Aung Tran) was one of my former, gregarious Vietnamese English language students and still is a good friend and witness. He was quite happy to be given the adopted nickname, *Ricky* and at that time I had so many mixed multi-nationals in my class of Mongolians, Chinese, South Korean, Vietnamese and Cambodians etc. that it was the first name that came to my mind when he asked me for a suitable English name. Convenient and easy to remember! Having to go through the class register of all those lengthy foreign names could be quite a challenge so at times if they had nicknames it would help immensely. Whilst on-line, I was asked for help and advice about where his sister had disappeared. I never knew anything about his sister, as he had never mentioned his family to me before. It wasn't necessary anyway. His family hadn't received any news consistently for several years, which was troubling.

My on-line messenger readings had at that time proved to be receptive enough and this has certainly been the case for the Vietnamese I have met on my travels. That included either doing readings, occasionally and spontaneously whilst attempting to teach a full class of students. For Ricky, I certainly had an immediate link here and so I went with the flow and it was just like a running brook of pure energy. I was asked for advice about his missing sister and so did my best. I told him that I felt his sister was not in Vietnam but across the border, and I began to sense her teaching in Cambodia as I felt myself scouring a regional map in my mind. Adding to this, I was fortunate enough to be able to sense she was actually pregnant or certainly with a baby on the way. "Pregnant – my sister?" He responded, in a disbelieving way.

This information was not fully accepted by Ricky at the time and it was kind of unacceptable for the family's daughter to run away and get pregnant, but a few weeks later I got an excited text on my mobile saying that his sister had finally come home, had been teaching in Cambodia, and was indeed pregnant. It does seem hard to believe and at times I have to get my former students to remind me that such a successful and event did happen.

Following the reading online, I had advised him and his family to light candles and pray out loud to ask god to 'finally bring their daughter home' in a dynamic, emotional and passionate manner in a unified way. This was not just to hope, but pray and say it out loud with gusto from the heart as a desperate plea and as a family.

Although I was not absolutely sure it was going to happen and not normally accustomed to being creative with personal prayer, it certainly felt that is was worth the effort. Their daughter incredibly returned within a few weeks straight out of the blue.

Wouldn't it be comforting to know that the advice was a result of being spiritually influenced and inspired? I certainly felt satisfaction from the event and so did Ricky and the family who, to this day I am still in contact with and will also never forget and always cherish the event. I have made quite a few long-term friendships this way and value it immensely, getting a great deal of satisfaction out of it when it proves to be successful.

Two years later Ricky was persuaded to contact me again directly by his family. His aunt had now passed over and the mother in particular, wanted to know what had happened to the estate. I hadn't realised that the arranged meeting was due to the fact that two years ago I had previously given Ricky a brief reading in a coffee shop in Saigon. I also hadn't expected to be put under pressure for such an important task. Ricky brought to my attention that I had originally mentioned his Aunt had passed away at that time and had left money to his family, which was quite substantial.

At that time he could not make sense of it, as she was still alive, in reasonably good health and living down the road! In fact, she was living around the corner – something else I had *not* known at the time. So what was the confusion, was it just a total gaff? No, I had not been aware that whilst sitting at that little coffee shop in a tree-lined boulevard on the top floor, overlooking that leafy street, that we were just a hundred metres from his Aunt's home.

Furthermore, I had mentioned that I felt she had passed over but I subsequently learnt that this didn't happen until actually only a few months after the reading. So she did actually pass over but not until two months later. Had I been sitting directly in front of her perhaps I may have been able to sense her imminent passing but of course, certainly would not have mentioned it. I think we can all pick up vibes like this in times of impending bereavement just like animals do. Time loops can sometimes be hard to decipher within mediumship for which I will explain next as it becomes a little clearer.

Meanwhile, for a further spiritual reading to clarify more about Ricky's aunt passing away, we arranged to meet at my hotel, a nice well-known one in China Town and central in Singapore amongst the former colonial architecture. I was now refreshed despite the jet lag and had just arrived from The UK two days previously.

Ricky was always enthusiastic with the spiritual world and psychic phenomena, so that helped add a kind of spiritual ambience to the reading so I decided to open with angel cards. I am not particularly astrologically minded or a Tarot expert, but these are the cards I prefer. It's like using a musical instrument – I eventually chose the piano over the drums and guitar as it felt better for me and I am more adept at it. I usually only do this method to 'warm up' then focus on the sixth sense or any messages that may come through on 'the other channel' which is my term for the psychic and clairvoyant energy or unconscious. Others may work differently and that's their prerogative, this happens to be mine.

I decided to attempt the clairvoyant reading at a coffee shop down town. I was quite sure that it had to be a specific coffee bar and not anywhere – that was the feeling or hunch again and we don't want to ignore that too often. As we were searching for a suitable place in the midday heat and sweaty, Singaporean humidity I felt that we had to turn and go back to an area of a very long street where we had already passed. Ricky was asking why we had to go back and I said it was where I knew it just *felt* right. We turned back despite walking past several other inviting, air-conditioned coffee bars and lounges along the way.

As we walked into the coffee bar I immediately noticed the large, trendy chandelier glowing and flickering with an abnormal luminosity and pulsation, which is not the usual symptom of electrical malfunctions. I had only seen similar clips of this on film, which was similar to potential paranormal or poltergeist activity. However, this was gentler and certainly benign as there were no dishes flying through the air!

I said, "There you are Ricky! Look at the chandelier light – that has to be the sign your aunt is already here and guided us to this coffee lounge".

As we stood there focussing on the flickering chandelier, I asked the manager to confirm how many days it had been flickering with such a pulsation. She confirmed it had only just begun as we walked in, apologising for the inconvenience and 'malfunction'. Feeling comforted already by the thought that I now had a head start and spirit contact, we got to work. I was startled to see Ricky getting out his paperwork which his parents had meticulously prepared – A large A3 sheet of paper rolled into a tube which included his family tree, a map of a house and some other details all in Vietnamese. For one moment, I felt I was being set-up or even used as a detective. I suppose in one sense, it was psychic detective work. I hadn't expected this and was a bit cautious thinking how serious all of this was suddenly looking. It seemed his parents sent him on a mission.

With a burst of energy and inspiration, I suddenly asked Ricky to write down ten names in Vietnamese of people within the family and some who were not directly connected to the will in any way of the apparent family feud. This is something I had done before on occasions and also on the spur of the moment. It seems to work fine for me when I get the feeling of spontaneous spiritual energy.

As he was now writing the names in Vietnamese, I got the number 2, 3 and 10 and so immediately pointed out that those very numbers of named people were the ones who were linked to the will and estate. Ricky gasped in astonishment and excitement. It was indeed the second, third and tenth name on his list that I was able to highlight as being connected to the family. The rest of the names were not at all connected. He confirmed it. Despite the fact I couldn't read Vietnamese at the time, I considered this a 'hit' and further proof we were connected. I went with the flow again and was now able to describe visually the house where the Aunt had lived and received further descriptive information about the interior as I was being shown in and out the downstairs rooms and up the stairway with the images going through my mind.

I saw that the *will* had been handed over to a stepsister and was supposed to have been split to Ricky and his mother – not just the stepdaughter. It appeared that the stepdaughter had deliberately kept the rest of the family in the dark for ulterior motives and had managed to dupe his elderly aunt into getting a lions-share of the family savings. It was what the parents had felt all along and I was just doing the job of confirmation and verification. However, it is not something I feel comfortable with doing and since this event I have refrained from getting involved in family squabbles.

By the time we both left the coffee shop the pulsating of the chandelier lighting had already stopped. Since this last meeting,

I have had the chance to do further spontaneous readings in coffee shops also in Vietnam for acquaintances and their friends. There is a diversity of these coffee shops and their popularity has spread all over the city in each of the districts. These have some kind of spiritual and psychic ambience to them for me and I enjoy the opportunity of sitting drinking a cappuccino tucked away off the main streets. It's also a habit of many local residents, young lovers, businessman and teens, who like to meet after work or in their free time. Some of these coffee shops are hidden in small alleys, others are quite flash and fashionable and always a great place to sit and relax and of course I select the most suitable spot to begin a reading.

If I had my way I would get up and play the piano too in between doing a reading! However, certain background music can be irritating if it's too loud and naturally is usually a distraction to the psychic and spiritual reception. Ironically, having said that, I have been able to sense specific personal information from a stranger in a disco! It is also said in psychic and spiritual circles that to raise the vibrations, singing or music helps with attracting communication. Well, as long as it's not heavy metal music then I should be able to get a psychic link at least. Then again, if you had known a heavy metal fan as a close friend or relative and *lost* them to the other side, then played the music at a reading at high volume, would this create the conditions for a more positive contact? Nothing is impossible.

There is also the theory that if it's not spiritual then it's possibly psychic and as a result of just being directly within a person's aura. However, I rule nothing out and this is on the basis that we understand that we all have auras too, for which there is enough evidence. Most spiritual circles and groups cover classes involving the study of the aura and I have taken part myself. There are many dimensions to the entire spiritual world and it would seem they all inter-connect in one form or another.

Chapter 7
A Lost Brother from Beyond

Living alone in another country, away from your family, culture and friends, including all those little luxuries of your original home country can have an odd effect on many of us. All those comforts we took for granted. All the important factors contribute to how we adjust to our well being, our emotional psyche and stability. I am sure this sparked at least one of the following experiences.

Periods of isolation away from home can awaken the spirit within you – especially if it is long periods of time as it was for me, almost two years at a time sometimes. At least, this is what it felt for me. Not that I sat and watched a sunrise on the desert dunes, with legs crossed in meditation – but time certainly can go incredibly slowly, depending on where you are exactly located in The Middle East. I don't describe my students in this chapter, as due to the cultural and religious ramifications, I resisted even the discussion of the spiritual and psychic in the classroom.

I did attempt it once but was ridiculed by a student in the front row of desks who said, "It is all in your imagination!" That stopped it right from going anywhere within the classroom here! I was on my guard from now on and besides I didn't want to allow my abilities to be scorned at. In any case, within the classroom teaching my Arabic students English, I did not seem to be psychically in-tune so much and therefore did not feel the need to open up in that way as I have done in The Far East and elsewhere.

So here I was now teaching in The Middle East. It was here that I began to have a spiritual awakening or *calling* from the other side for which I hadn't realised at the time. Whilst at lunch, one day sitting at the lunch table with another teaching colleague I was approached by a mature Irish man, greying at the temples, who had been in the gulf working a while – or as we say 'been around the block in the trade'.

Brendan took me by surprise, as he immediately and eagerly asked me in his crisp and clear Southern Irish accent "Jonny, I hear you are psychic and I wonder if you could help me? You see, it's my brother…"

As Brendan hovered over the table with his bushy-grey eyebrows slightly twitching, he focused his eyes on me with eager alertness anticipating my response, as he clutched an empty water glass on the table with a slice of lemon in it. As the bubbles fizzed in his glass, I remained composed and unruffled. I was stabbing at a piece of dried salad and humous pitta with olives, but alert and empathetic enough despite having to get up at 5am which seemed to be the norm here – at least it was for us teachers.

Then Suddenly, I got alarm bells, and a sudden feeling of blackness, which at that time felt to be distinctively crime related. The information although brief was swift – I immediately sensed a specific location and clearly the name of his brother's doctor, which was a traditional Irish name and a potential country which he had likely fled to, or been connected with. Brendan had not seen his brother for ten years.

He confirmed his worst thoughts that there was indeed something crime related, lowered his head slightly as if in deep solemn thought, looking to the floor. For some reason, I was prompted to ask him to consult his brother's doctor who may know something more.

We left it there and in the evening late after work as I relaxed, sitting composed on the sofa I decided to say a heart-felt prayer for both of them – both Brendan and his lost brother. I needed more information but this occurrence, experience and development was fairly new to me so I did what I felt was right out of compassion. It almost began to feel like a compelling duty and a spiritual one. Sometimes we need no words or have none to describe such a situation or feeling like this.

I immediately saw the name 'SEAN' and repeatedly the same location as the day before, plus a Southern Irish town and also one in the Northern Province. I quickly wrote it all down on a small pocket-sized note-pad. Next day, and it was a damn hot, sweltering one at that, set in the arid desert heat and blinding sunlight, I approached Brendan who was on his way to the photocopying room in the adjoining cabin which were set a few hundred yards from the much larger classroom cabins.

Firmly clutching the piece of paper from the night before, I was a little hesitant and felt my heart beat quicker as to how I may feel if I was incorrect at this stage. Adding to that, I didn't want my reputation tarnished by encouraging others to promote what some sceptics would perceive as a 'nut' on the campus! However, I felt an overwhelming urge to convey the information I received and get it over with.

"Brendan, may I have a word with you? I think I have something for you but I am not 100% sure." I asked, hesitatingly. My confidence a little self-doubting, he responded in a swift, no-nonsense but affable down to earth Irish manner, "Sweet Jesus, just give it to me."

I read out and showed the crumpled piece of paper in my hand. "Brendan," I said hesitantly, "I have the name 'Sean' and two specific named locations here." Showing him the paper, I asked him if it made any sense to him. He was shocked. It was the actual name of his long lost brother and the towns I'd written down he confirmed made total sense to him, including the suspected area of his brother's last whereabouts all those years ago. It made my heart beat a little faster too knowing

I was correct on this occasion. Of course, it isn't always like this but when it is, it leaves us feeling blessed.

I left for class and let it rest. However, it soon got around the office and campus, the rest of the teaching staff and co-workers who began to think I was either a nut or someone to tease, if not bully. I had to deal with the skeptical backlash from a few unsavoury characters. Needless to say I managed to get through it all and avoid the negative responses and behaviour by those who wished not to believe in such occurrences and those who chose to ridicule despite the evidence. I learnt a lesson about being too open to help people and it wasn't easy. I had to deny a lot to protect myself.

It amazes me how people here in this physical dimension are still too quick to mock factual accounts of the spiritual even when they have witnesses. In small work circles overseas people tend to talk more about others they know, hence circulating gossip which can work against you, becoming exaggerated and occasionally spiteful. Although that little bit of information I was fortunate to pluck from spirit may not be dynamic evidence for some, it certainly made Brendan take notice. As for the sudden potential of having a link with his lost and possibly deceased brother I believe the information *was* relayed from beyond to me. He had needed verification of whether he had indeed passed over although this delicate matter wasn't discussed between us as I was just beginning to discover and make sense of this phenomena myself.

I hadn't known at the time that certain information regarding my psychic aptitude was getting around the workplace. It did surprise me to be approached by someone I barely knew which involved a rather personal and delicate matter from a co-worker who had lost contact with their brother. Furthermore, it surprised me that I was able to produce personal evidence boosting my confidence to consider more seriously what I had the potential to do with god's assistance.

Middle East Blues

It was another, regular blistering afternoon and I was sheltering in my air-conditioned room as usual on the weekend off. Not many venture out in the mid-day sweltering heat in The Middle East unless you've got a nice air-conditioned vehicle at your disposal, or you just happen to be unlucky – don't believe me? Try it and see – hah! The tyres of the cars can actually melt there and certainly the road tarmac softens. You can cook eggs on the bonnet of a car. You will know what heat really feels like when you are in the gulf in the afternoon!

I remember how naïve I was the day I went out for an afternoon walk across the bone dry wasteland to stock up with a new drum of drinking water which meant I had to carry it all the way back. It was the only way to get to the *Bukala*, the small food store across the rubble and desert dust as not all of us had a vehicle –sometimes this was shared on different days anyway. I barely made it, almost flaked out and had to recuperate plopping down onto a large rice carton for support under the shops faltering, over-worked air-conditioner whilst I recovered.

Heading back with a rapidly, melting choc-ice trickling down the sides of my hand and a gallon drum of purified water, I suddenly felt the compelling need to call my good Thai friend, in Bangkok. On arrival to my apartment the signal strength on my mobile phone was weak so I went up to the open-rooftop of our apartment block where the water tanks were located. I found a spot with a view among the haphazardly placed Satellite dishes in the baking heat with connecting cables entwined like spaghetti on the whole of the rooftop. I found a shady, sheltered area and proceeded to dial my phone. My friend, Zack answered his mobile almost immediately and seemed unusually surprised to hear from me at that time.

"How did you know?" he said eagerly. "Know what?" I responded.

Zack went on to let me know he was now at the funeral of his close tour-guide friend. It was Nat his good friend and co-work colleague. He had been brutally murdered and his body was dumped in a plastic sack following suffocation and strangulation. A tremendous waste of a young life I couldn't help but immediately pray for his spirit. I felt numb, emotional and sullen, as I had been introduced to him only two months prior to briefly meeting.

The 'sick', sombre feeling that came over me was partly due to the fact that even though I had not known him as a personal friend there were warning bells earlier on that I had sensed. This was on the very first day I was introduced to him in the small travel agent's office. As we were walking along the busy and noisy, Bangkok Street in the rush hour, I suddenly had this odd but clear thought that came into my mind. I turned and looked at Nat directly amongst the noise of the rush hour, I recall clearly saying that he 'has to take care' where he is going as I felt he was just not safe at all. This *was* a strange message for me to give as I was not accustomed to forwarding messages of a warning kind and especially to someone I didn't know well. I felt what made me say that? It was nagging at me and I could not make sense of it. Think about it –how would you feel having the sudden need to warn someone that concerned a future, potential tragedy to a stranger, which may sound bizarre and ominous?

Nat, unperturbed in response, smiled widely and said that he was going 'up to the north' to be near his family that weekend and was looking forward to it. My rational, logical mind was to think that he should be fine going to stay near his family but my 'other' irrational, if not unconscious mind said something was wrong and I felt uneasy.

After hearing my friend on the phone inform me of his brutal death, of course, I felt devastated for him by not having or maintaining a stronger link at the time. I had wished I'd been perceptive enough to express it in a much more influential, emphatic and vital manner. What an understatement. Perhaps it was fate and a sense of impending doom that I was feeling. It has to be taken into account that at that time I was experiencing something, which I had not realised was a 'gift' or even a message from spirit in its early and involuntary development stage. On hearing of his tragic death I shed a tear for someone I did not actually know apart from a brief introduction and immediately said a passionate prayer for his soul, for which I know, was sadly too late. Some say 'Rest in Peace'. But I don't believe someone so active, energetic and young whose life was cut short so soon would be resting. And do we rest as soon as we pass? That is another interesting question for which views will differ.

It certainly wasn't always rosy teaching. I had taught mostly young adults in a Middle-Eastern country, which I prefer to keep nameless and I visited several. In one particular case I was obliged to fail an adult student in an examination. This seemed to be unacceptable for him to take in front of his classmates since he had always felt he was the most successful. Losing face was intolerable for him as he had a personal reputation to maintain. He felt was he was the best in the class therefore having to demonstrate it verbally for some reason. We had always got along well up until this period, so the day this student taunted me about the disappearance of my cat with a wide, sadistic grin on his face was telling and quite shocking. With chest pushed out like a pigeon, arms proudly folded in front of him and acting in a suspicious manner, he smugly grinned again and turned to his friends. They most obviously knew what had been done to the beautiful, young cat, which had only just grown out of its kitten hood. I hadn't told anyone up to that time about its gruesome death.

 I tried to hold my feelings inside but it was evident following investigations that my adopted Siamese-blue Kitten (a very young, adopted office cat) had been heinously attacked with what appeared to be some kind of slow-burning battery acid.

Its skin and fur had melted to the bone. This experience of teaching in the gulf and witnessing the ill treatment of animals (especially dogs) had a profound effect on me. I had come across much worse stories but felt mine worthy to mention.

I and another work-colleague took it to the vets as it cried in agony and had been this way for at least three days before we had noticed. It had been suffering during a public holiday whilst we were away for an extended break as the school buildings where we worked were locked. We had left enough pet food for a week but it could not eat or drink. It's an experience I can't forget and tragically we let the vet put it to sleep with his advice. I was so fond of the Siamese, which used to roll around on the office chair to the gentle, mellow humming of a Buddhist chant on the CD player.

In my view, there has to be something as logical as Karma to reciprocate pain and suffering that one inflicts on others, and that includes god's creatures.

Chapter 8

Rest in Peace?

'RIP' on headstones has been a common and ubiquitous inscription for many centuries. Resting in peace for some that have passed away may indeed be a myth as I have already mentioned. One of my misadventures as a teen was experimenting with the infamous Ouija board. I am certainly not advising or recommending others to experiment with such a tool without being aware of the possible negative implications if one meddles. Would you call up an undesirable stranger from an unknown location who resided in a potentially hostile environment? Adding to that, to say "how are you doing and come on in?". Let alone, one you couldn't see. In effect, that is what you could be doing if left to the novice and unaware, enquiring mind.

However, from amongst all the initial, futile information I had encountered, were some very true facts and even predictions. However, putting biblical or religious views aside, for which I don't discount all of them, I do stress that it is not to be used for idle entertainment. There are energies that can affect the state of the mind, which I believe links directly to the vaults of the unconscious. We are after all, multisensory beings and can connect in a variety of ways as channels but this needs more caution.

Our consciousness needs to connect with *higher*, angelic sources and the Ouija board in my opinion does not always offer this immediately – if at all – which can at times be quick to manipulate and keep the intrepid recipient fascinated and in some cases, obsessed. It could have the potential to keep our attention for nothing useful until influential, obsessive behaviours set in. I can't prove it but I had at one time experienced it myself to a certain extent as a teenager. Some have had nightmares using this method of spiritual communication.

I was often engaged in conversations with 'personalities' using the Ouija board. Some were long drawn out conversations, which occasionally went on for days, but others were very brief and only lingered for an hour or so. In one case, my friend and I were given a Germanic-Jewish sounding name in origin from the period of the Second World War. My brief communications through the Ouija would sound almost a sinister joke if it were not a reality of the sheer terrors that actually occurred looking back to the events under the command of the infamous and heinous Nazis. We were told in our communication on how spirit had died by affirming he had been gassed to death in The Harz Mountains in Germany.

Naturally, my friend and I checked the map and eventually located it but at that time didn't commit to researching whether there had indeed been any information about concentration camps. Attempting to prise more salient points became laborious and at times the link seemed to throw so many incomprehensible sentences. At other times we went back to the Ouija board a week later only to resume the communication with the same personality we had previously. We were given military language used by the army personnel of that time and other relevant, connected information but not enough to have kept our permanent attention.

We could say there are similarities here with mediumship as the energies come and go with information. At times the 'personality' seemed to even become bored with us intrepid recipients of such probing information! There are others who say that we can be tricked into receiving information from false spirits in order to get our attention. I wouldn't disagree with this either. I was more interested in extracting hard facts for which I had later been able to prove. Some were realised at a much later date such as names of people, dates, places etc.

Whatever the case, it is truly an impressive phenomenon when one achieves credible information of this nature, which could not have otherwise been a mere chance. This is especially more significant where someone hadn't had any previous historical and specific, geographical knowledge of such locations or people's lives. Looking back, had I possessed the maturity and insight that I have now, I wish I had kept a meticulous diary of the more stimulating spiritual communications I had experienced. That is a far more worthy point to note instead of having to reminisce over those significant moments. This may be regrettable but this was the way it was and I can't alter it.

The communications were usually by me and another local student friend to sit with. We had at times become rather obsessed with the events but I am glad it eventually all ended, as I felt drained mentally after long periods experimenting with the Ouija. In effect, it almost became a compulsion. I am sure even I myself, wanted credible proof, wanting to avoid being gullible and to have as much evidence as I could. As a teenager, in those days my geography and acquaintance with facts would have been less prolific than as an adult. Particularly World War history was not a main part of the curriculum in my school life. I was <u>not</u> unaware of specific World War Two history or even World War One –and quite rightly so.

However, one unusual experience occurred to me as a small child, of which the memory remains with me to this day as clear as crystal. I distinctively recall being in hospital whilst only a mere five-year-old with tonsillitis. I was quite disturbed by some unsettling vision and feeling that I was sensing whilst I lay in that little hospital bed as a small child. The Catholic nuns who worked at the hospital were also nurses and often sitting at the bottom of the bed attentively but didn't stay long. At visiting time, I uncharacteristically asked my brother if the German soldiers were coming to attack the hospital to 'get us'. They were surely coming and I can see the image now as they stoop and run across the street and up the steps in their uniforms, carrying their weaponry.

What an imagination one may say. However, in the late Seventies that would not be a rational fear for a five-year-old unless a child had been repeatedly exposed to audio-visual or reading material on a consistent basis for which I hadn't. The Second World War ended in 1945 as we know. I am also not sure if there was a rational explanation as to why I thought we were still at war up until the age of about six! The feelings and images slowly disappeared after that age. Again, in The nineteen seventies at around the age of only five it would not be plausible to have a rational fear of this nature – even as a child in my opinion. I am not necessarily implying an explanation of a past life in ALL cases of children's 'imagination' but highlighting similarities of unexplained fears and memories, which could be indicative of them. It is not unknown for children all over the world to talk about factual experiences from unknown sources, which do not make sense concerning their existing environment or upbringing. There is plenty of information of this nature circulating for all to see. Some of you may also have your own experiences so I am sure mine isn't an isolated case.

Needless to say, that It wasn't until later with the access to the Internet, which made it so convenient that I made the effort to actually confirm the specific information about The Harz Mountains. I had not known anything specifically about such locations, but only later discovered factual evidence about concentration camps where the Jewish population were incarcerated in that region.

As for the concept of time, and the small but significant predictions I received for my own personal life, it can't be comprehended fully and in spiritual terms it is often said that only the 'now' exists.

It's a possibility in the physical sense; there could be a time loop or what some call a time warp. If this was not the case, we have to consider how I could have been given detailed facts including names, periods of time as far as ten years or more into the future. Certainly, the information may not have included large chunks of what was to happen in between the spaces of time and dates given, however, it did indeed uncover some specific and significant moments in time and events later on.

As a teenager, I had eagerly asked a member of the local UFO group if I may be able to 'have a go' in communicating with whatever comes up using the Ouija or cosmic conscious. Yes, a few of our local UFO group members were also deeply interested in the spiritual realm too, as we met in a three-story Victorian house in Wales. As the nights got darker at the end of the autumn, we would sit around a warm log fire drinking hot cups of tea, exchanging thoughts on the afterlife and similar stimulating topics. Often we would have a guest practice some kind of mind reading activity or as a group, develop a variety of clairvoyant exercises.

One theory is that the Ouija is not always direct spiritual contact but can also be from the unconscious super-mind. I recall asking a simple question whether I would be moving house or not. A simple question but significant for me. I was given a specific date, month and year, which continued to add two names of friends and acquaintances I would meet in the future in the new location. Nothing so unusual you may say except that, in fact the communication went on to spell out how long my family would be staying at the next location before moving onto another house move even later! Since I hadn't at that stage moved in my entire lifetime I was skeptical and made it known often in the sitting. That is not always a good response to give especially if an obliging spirit contact is attempting to answer our questions with clarity and compassion, but then I was a kid. I have moved a least ten times since that prediction.

These communications would lead us to accept there is some kind of separate personality or entity with a consciousness. The glass or planchette as we call it seemed to display annoyance as it spun vigorously in response to my skepticism. The name *Luke* was spelt out first and was followed quickly by *Alex*, second. The small glass spun around and repeated '*Luke*' emphatically several times as I challenged the information by saying, 'I very much doubt it!' Yes, even I was a skeptic at one time – a naive novice and unaware of the physical and non-physical elements feeling more at home with the rational world. The glass bobbed back and fore whilst repeating and focusing on two specific letters and a related name –'*MS*' *LUKE*. I had thought it meant *I would meet a 'Luke' in a famous department store*, which share the same initials.

I put all that aside despite the fact that I was also given information that I would be teaching in the Far East ten years later. Of course I ignored it, I was not one to believe in what I had felt to be most unlikely or implausible especially as at that stage in life I hadn't possessed a University degree or teaching qualifications. I neither had envisaged myself to be joining such a profession, or yet mature enough and achieving such qualifications in the future. How wrong I was! That all changed and of course I was fortunate to go to University later.

A few years later following the 'Ouija board reading' my parents had by then moved home twice. It was here at a small house-warming party my parents were giving that I was introduced to a young guy who I was asked to meet. He had arrived with his mother and father from the nearby farm. I amicably introduced myself in the informal way. His name was Luke. I hadn't immediately realised it but this boy; aged 17 was in the early diagnosed stages of Multiple Sclerosis otherwise termed as MS.

Luke was only just recently getting used to his crutches and was propped up in the doorway with a big friendly grin on his face. He gave me a big welcoming 'How yah doing?' Luke was beginning to wear glasses for his sight, which was affected by his condition. To be struck down at this age for a young and otherwise fit and healthy young guy was not only obviously disabling but quite frustrating and upsetting too. And here I was, several years on from that earlier prediction with a new friend called Luke. But who was Alex?

On a backpacking adventure throughout the USA I was given an address in Portland, Oregon State, by Luke's parents. I duly paid a visit to Luke's brother. His name was Alex. Sadly, over the next few years, Luke's condition deteriorated. We got on very well and although his diagnosed condition was now worsening and his sight failing rapidly he managed to put on a brave and positive face. I had always intended to cheer him up on my visits and we were of a similar age group. Music was something we both shared with similar tastes. We only had one disagreement, concerning the subject of Karma and reincarnation!

Remarkably, a few years on whilst teaching overseas in the Middle East, I was sat in the school office with a teaching Colleague, Ray. It was scorching heat outside and just a desert wasteland, a small mosque and shop could be seen through the shades in the distance. It was a time of the day for some reason or another that the new students hadn't yet arrived. It was indeed a peaceful opportunity to have a chat about life and the world with a coffee, considering having to be up so early – at the crack of dawn, actually.

A vivid thought suddenly came into my mind just at that moment. As we sipped our freshly made coffee, I began to describe the life quite vividly of Luke to Ray who sat there attentively. I began to talk about and describe whilst seeing distinct images, memories and of the stories Luke had told me when he had been more able-bodied. One fascinating event in his life included the time in Kenya, Africa, where his family had been posted temporarily. He had waded into the river as a child to unhook his fishing line. He thought it had become caught in some undergrowth and had decided to free it. Just in the nick of time Luke spotted a pair of large, reptilian eyes protruding from the water. Suddenly he realised it was a crocodile, which was floating spread-eagled just below the water but with the eyes slightly above water level with strategic intent. The Crocodile had been waiting for him to retrieve the entangled line and therefore have a quick and easy meal! He had never run so fast out of water in his life and of course, fortunately survived to tell the tale so I could let everyone else know!

So here I was, far away from home, unusually reminiscing about Luke's life in the school office when now the phone suddenly rang. It was my father. Luke had just died and his mother had called our family to let us know, as we were close friends. I was shocked if not only for the timing alone and it didn't stop there. Within moments of the call with the awful news a whiteboard marker shot directly vertically into the air and across the room landing on the table. Ray and I were both startled. "Did you see what I just saw?" I gasped.

Of course, we both witnessed it and agreed that we had no idea how a whiteboard marker could fly up in the air and across the room and land on my desk for both of us to see! We attempted to re-enact the experience using the white-board marker to see how it would be possible through normal physical means. We both agreed that it was most likely to be Luke's presence and his way of letting me know he was there.

Think about it. It was not typical or indeed even occasional for me to mention Luke let alone his entire life, his situation and character as I had just done so that moment. I had lost touch with him for several years whilst on my overseas teaching assignments and my life went in a different direction since moving location. But here I was, finally telling a teaching colleague his life story, which simultaneously and remarkably resulted with an almost synchronized phone call announcing his passing over. I am sure I was receptive to his spirit on that occasion and that Luke was making himself known to let me know he was thinking of me. I am often reminded from a former American lecturing friend who once said to me – "Coincidences of which there are none".

Chapter 9

Contact on a Plane: Jewellery and Missing Items

Subsequently, I was advised on a training for mediumship course, along with other students to 'sense any potential' that may manifest in the future of the person who we are giving a reading. In effect this is the essence of what I had tried but failed to convey fully to Nat, the young man from Thailand who lost his life in such a horrendous way. One of my own particular abilities, which I have come across without books or guidance, is the sensing of a person's lifeline. For me, this is where I am able to feel specific events and changes of significance in a person's life from a very early age, sometimes from birth. This could be months, dates, years or periods of time in transition.

I can give an example of the time I gave a reading on an airplane. This was for a woman who had lost her husband at the age of 40 for which I will go into detail a little later and for which our meeting proved to be another unusual timing. As we recall, 'coincidences of which there are none' or at least, few. I was able to pick up the month and year of her daughter's birth, her marriage, graduation from University and the time she began her first job. These datelines are all significant events within a person's lifeline.

It should be noted that tuning into a person's energy field either with or without direct spirit help is not immediately identifiable but in this case of the lady on the plane incident, I can say the help would have most likely come from her husband's spirit. I also knew there had to be a reason for her to be sitting exactly next to me in row 55. I was 55a and she, 55b. To give us a clue why I believe there was a reason I will elaborate.

There was an interesting occurrence three days prior to the flight. I was choosing my seat on the airline website at short notice and adjusted it three times to a different seat before it mysteriously re-arranged it back to the original seat number in row 55. In fact by the fourth time it wouldn't budge from 55 on the online seat-locator system! I tried, then gave up and left it as the original choice. Perhaps this was influenced by spirit. However, I often say to others not to reject anything that may be plausible but there seemed to be a computer glitch here or something else. That 'something else' was unusual as the online system did let me alter it but I had later mysteriously moved it back to the seat number I had originally chosen.

We shouldn't dismiss some of the unexplainable either, that may leave us perplexed and for which the rational can just never explain. Sylvana, the woman sitting next to me was well-dressed in black and with a full Italian name to boot, certainly could have been a stereotype, Italian widow in mourning – excusing the Australian accent as in this case, she was Australian but of Italian descent.

I had boarded the plane from Singapore ready for the 13-hour or more endurance. I was in a three-seat row. The woman was dressed ironically in black. She politely squeezed into the seat next to me and between another passenger on her left side. Often I don't wish to chat immediately on planes, as on long-haul flights you could be worn out, if not sick of each other by the time you get to your destination! I prefer to save my energy and wind down for a peaceful trip. I've done this flying endurance too often. However, I was already involuntarily tuning in as I felt this person's presence and energy field despite not having spoken yet. Psychics do this intentionally for planned sittings but there was a good reason for it this time despite it not being planned by me.

I just knew that she was someone who was open, not a skeptic or a cynic and would be able to accept things of a spiritual matter, particularly regarding life after death – if not a reading to go with it. I wondered how I could enter into a conversation about this topic with the other passenger and stranger sitting immediately on her left side. I imagined myself saying. 'Excuse me, I'm a psychic who is picking up information from you'... and 'may I go ahead and do a reading?' I didn't think so somehow. So how was I going to do it?

Here I was on a plane and I could just feel that spiritual buzz, vibrations, presence – the knowing that the person next to me was open to the topic of life on the other side and something active from the spirit world was going on around her. Those particularly involved in the spiritual business will share and understand what I mean quite clearly. So what was I to say? I thought best to wait until I cornered her when she went to the washroom. Yes, that's the best thing to do, I decided; at least there should be less people around there on this 747 Jet. Best to do this before the meals are served, I thought.

There was no need to explain myself. Sylvana, almost immediately began the introductory chat by telling me her husband had died one year previously and had wanted her to do this trip.

An unusual introductory chat line I thought, but I believe family spirit also can influence and stimulate thoughts of necessity to produce desired results. They just don't wait. This is especially true if there is a more timely opportunity to do so, as it was in this case.

I said to myself – 'that's the sign and that's the key'. Not many would normally open a conversation to a total stranger with personal information such as this; by telling me a deceased partner told them to make this trip! –Well, most wouldn't as it's personal. As I listened carefully, she told me her husband was only 40 when he passed over with cancer.

I knew something spiritually active was going on already. She was now out of her seat by the restroom area and so I felt this was an opportunity to be equally open with her about the spiritual vibe I was sensing. I mentioned to her that I had psychic abilities and hoped she didn't mind me doing a reading of some kind for her. She was so obligingly open and eager to talk as she had actually once been to a professional psychic after her husband's death. However, she was also cautious and certainly not gullible.

As we flew over the Himalayas, I approached her discreetly outside the restrooms away from potential eavesdroppers. Fortunately, she was enthusiastic for any information I might be able to pick up. During the reading, I was able to visualise that the lights in one of her bedrooms had recently been flickering, going on and off intermittently which included the television. All of this for no apparent or logical reason but for which I was able to convey that her husband's spirit had not intended to cause a scare. Sylvana, uttered an 'oh my god' with her hands covering her mouth as her eyes lit up, whilst the flight attendant squeezed passed us with soft-drinks, looking our way and bending her ear with eager curiosity. Sylvana promptly confirmed that she had indeed been experiencing electrical interference and her daughter had not only felt but had also seen an image of her deceased father in the bedroom standing at the foot of the bed. The experience did scare the daughter but this is not usual and his message was that it was not the intention and he apologised!

Sylvana agreed with me and understood that when energies mingle with our physical dimension sometimes the vibrations affect the electrical supply. On some rare occasions this has been known to blow bulbs and fuses. She had done her homework too about the afterlife but still wanted more proof, which is understandable. Fortunately, although I continued to confirm several friends and family members around her it wasn't until the plane was due to land that I felt prompted to ask her another question. I needed to hold a personal item of Sylvana's that may enable me to sense something more significant. I felt it might give some real concrete evidence of her husband's presence. I asked politely for her ring, which she gladly but carefully, removed from her finger and placed into my hand.

Some professionals in the psychic business call this psychometry and for me it helps when I need to tune in more with the person I am sitting with and attempting to read. Almost instantly I clutched her ring and held it in my fingers I was able to feel and therefore say 'He's showing me Swansea, Wales'. She held her breath placing her hand onto her chest with fingers spread in a fan of shock. I watched her eyes open wide like a child who had opened Pandora's Box, except it should have been me with the same expression. Swansea, Wales in the United Kingdom made a whole lot of sense as it was the exact location where she and her husband were when they chose the ring I was now holding.

I immediately asked her to confirm if she was aware of the connection of 'Argyle Hampton' in Wales, UK'. 'My god, she said, why absolutely, it was the name of the jewellers store we were both in when my husband bought it and we had hunted for the right one everywhere until we found it'. Sylvana was flabbergasted which made me feel so jubilant that I had a real breakthrough and the confirmation she had needed as evidence, which only her husband on the other side could have passed on from spirit and ever known.

I feel that a spirit often likes to finish and give a little kick of attention especially when they know the medium and recipient are due to leave. They like to get a message across, as it may be their only chance. After all, it's not a daily occurrence to meet and be in a situation like this. Meanwhile, I left Sylvana feeling more content than she had been for a long time and that is comforting to know. It was the ring that her husband had bought, and so the sentimental, nostalgic attachment to a personal possession became the life bonding experience that only Sylvana could have experienced. Certainly nobody else on the plane would have known the facts of where exactly the ring was bought. This was bought at a significant and memorable time in both Sylvana's and her 'deceased' husband's life. This was the crucial enough evidence to convince her. I feel there can be no ignorance of real facts and we were both lucky on this occasion.

Having said that, it is widely believed amongst mediums and psychics that spirit is constantly present around loved ones in one way or another. If not only waiting for the right moment to contact but also actually attempting to influence a connection or situation that leads to a favourable result. So perhaps there was a reason for me to be sitting in row fifty-five after all despite me attempting on several occasions to alter it.

It's not unknown for a loved one in spirit to have known the bereaved family members were going to be having a meeting with a medium in advance and this includes the destination or location they would be heading to. This could indicate that spirit does have some involvement in the action to get them to that stage or it may draw us back to the 'time' issue and the ability to see the future before those of us in this physical world are able to. Even if it is at twenty-five thousand feet in an airplane – this doesn't seem to matter.

A little jade stone

Still on the subject of psychometry and personal objects, I add this recent experience. For the skeptic and 'Doubting Thomas' of this world, this is someone I met who had an item of jewellery and the connection to the spirit world. Enter Mr Siva. No, not a spirit entity from the other dimension! Siva was my former educational observer whilst teaching overseas. An amiable, congenial gentleman, Singaporean and mature in years, who would certainly not let anyone including a psychic or medium pull the wool over his eyes. On a return visit through Asia I called him up and asked if he would actually like to chat about education, but I thought I'd also throw in a card reading. In this case, mine were angel cards as opposed to Tarot. Tarot isn't for everyone and can sometimes be quite intense in my view, but there is a combination of imagery and intuition in both.

For me, these angel cards tend to focus more on spiritual advice in a positive way without giving too much of a scare. I often open with cards to tune in as a warm up, as back up and a gentle connector to the other side should spirit attempt to assist with accompanying information. However, Mr Siva was not one to be scared off and certainly worked by logic and the rational mind, but I had not known at the time that he was a 'doubting Thomas'. Just as well really.

We met at a downtown Indian vegetarian restaurant and over a refreshing, Indian-style ginger tea I told him to shuffle the cards, cut the deck and pick out the top three. Fortunately, all three cards were spot on and relevant to his current and past situation with the third apparently determining his future plans. He wasn't particularly ruffled yet, judging by his body language.

However, not long into the reading, I saw the image of an elderly Indian lady at the bottom of some steep stairs, who appeared to have had a fall in that exact spot. Siva promptly confirmed this by saying it had happened over fifteen years previously. But time is irrelevant – or at least our 'time' and how we relate it to the spiritual and the physical world.

Now sensing his mother draw nearer, I was shown head bandages and then delicately had to let him know I was seeing something, which may be delicate and upsetting. It was clear – the words 'brain haemorrhage'. I made it clear that was exactly what I saw, despite feeling uncomfortable about saying it, as this could be an upsetting memory.

Siva became suddenly quiet as he cleared his throat and appeared lost for words, a little out of breath as he whispered the confirmation that his mother did specifically pass over with that very condition of a brain haemorrhage due to a fall to the bottom of the stairs. There was more, spirit was able to give me two months, which were specific to an accident – February and July. Why was this I pondered? How can it be both February and July? Surely it had to be either one or the other? I thought I was going to look a fool, as the gap between February and July was a large one.

Quite simply Siva went onto confirm that his mother had been taken into the hospital in February and passed over in July. I wanted to keep up the communication so I asked if I could hold his gold ring, which was adorned with a variety of colourful and special stones –in fact there were nine on this multi-stone ring and each was relevant to the lunar calendar. This ring was therefore one that meant a great deal to him.

What's the issue with the ring then, I hear you say? Just as I was picking up information from his mother, I told Siva, I was trying as hard as I could to prise some more credible, personal details. I felt mental pressure to get some more information of substance about his mother. I felt a mild headache coming. At that immediate moment the small, precious jade stone (the ninth out of nine small stones) popped out of the ring setting, into the air and bounced onto the table like a tiny ping pong ball! He was as stunned as I was embarrassed. Here we were sitting in a restaurant with other guests brushing past our table and a family of diners sitting across from us now gazing our way with inquisitiveness through the leafy palm plants and large slits of a wooden trellis screen.

Embarrassed, wondering if I was going to be scolded that his wonderful prized ring of many years which had not left his finger for some considerable time, had become suddenly and unexplainably spoilt. 'Good Grief!' Siva uttered a gasp.

'It's not me, I said in a slight panic, I didn't touch it, it was balanced on my fingers –you saw that as a fact, right?'

Luckily for me, the gentlemanly but stunned Siva was more perplexed and intrigued than annoyed. Perplexed that a stone which had been engrained for so long and never been removed had suddenly, due to no physical pressure from either of us managed to free itself with gusto and bounce all over the restaurant table like a ping pong ball!

It reminded me of the days when as a teenager, I would hurry to a spiritual circle to meet all kinds of unusual people who were involved in similar unusual interests. As a child, this is where I met one clairvoyant who as a kind of mentor demonstrated to me and the group, metal bending of a spoon and fork, using apparent mind power. I had later after many attempts, been able to eventually reproduce the phenomena at home using a thick, silver back-door key. I was sitting in total silence and in my parent's old cottage at that time late in the evening. I concentrated on one side of the key for about five minutes by saying a short prayer to whomever or whatever may be listening. My heart started beating faster with palpitations as the opposite end of the key for which I put all my focussed effort into started to move upwards, and what a thrill I got out of that! I remember my reactions quite vividly. At that moment I thought if a physical object such as a key or cutlery could move from 'mind power' alone then science and the world as I had up to that day understood it, must be flawed. I then suddenly thought the world was my oyster for paranormal activity having not only witnessed it but being a real part of the experience.

Meanwhile, in the restaurant, we didn't lose the stone from Siva's ring and it didn't drop into an adjacent diner's meal or somewhere else embarrassing – thank heavens. All I can assume is that it was either telekinetic energy or his deceased mother's vibrations giving it one hell of a go to let her beloved son know she was around and truly doing her best to show it! That may after all be the only chance she got to make herself known to her son since passing over. He certainly can't forget his ring had never been off his finger for years or ever lost a stone previously. I can also say that prior to the stone suddenly popping out for no apparent reason, as the ring was balanced on the tips of my fingers and palm of the hand there was a real feeling of palpable energy.

Recently, I received a follow up email informing me that Siva had since lost the stone but that it re-appeared in an obscure place in the house. He firmly believed that the occurrences of the little jade stone and his mother were trying to tell him something. I have mentioned repeatedly for us not to disregard anything if it seems plausible and in this case, the spiritually feasible. It was also in this case, rewarding to make a 'Doubting Thomas' and former skeptic sit up and think for once.

Chapter 10

In the Classroom: A Snake and a Crucifix

Another spontaneous occurrence, which took place unexpectedly and included personal items of jewellery, concerned one of my former students in the classroom. I have had the fortune to teach many different nationalities over the years in multilingual classes from Vietnamese to Mongolians, Chinese to South Koreans and Italians to Russians.

Victor, an older student from East Timor was diligent and alert, of darker-complexion who appeared very introvert and timid. Sat at the back row of the classroom I had never seen him chat to any other students since the day he arrived like the others – well not inside the classroom. He certainly couldn't manage to muster up the confidence to get involved with any speaking activities despite his high test score and entrance paper in the English exam. However, it wasn't a lack of enthusiasm on his part at all. A committed and attentive student who obtained a scholarship, he attracted my attention as I sensed there was something troubling him or possibly some kind of emotional baggage from his past.

I have always been alert and incredibly sensitive to students' moods and feelings. But what was the psychic vibe I was now sensing from Victor? Indeed was it psychic intuition? I pondered this. We often say we have a hunch like the sixth sense or intuition but there was a little more to it here. I was actually experiencing another clairvoyant sensation in the classroom, which was not intended or encouraged simply just for the thrill of it. I also sensed Victor had gone through an immense and considerable amount of suffering. A trickle of sweat ran down my back from perspiration absorbing into my new shirt, caused by the tropical humidity.

I was irritated by a faulty, ineffective and noisy air-conditioner and there were gaps in the windows. The local mosquito fumigator was outside spraying his chemical treatment –dengue is widespread in parts of South Asia. I could feel the acrid taste building up in my mouth, as I held onto my whiteboard marker and text book in hand ready to address the class. I had a class full of fumes before from this chemical but I was still ordered to teach as the fumes gently seeped through the windows and formed into a light mist above the classroom.

As I was busily writing the past perfect tense on the whiteboard, I was now beginning to sense a grandfatherly or paternal presence around Viktor dressed in what seemed like blue gardening or industrial overalls. The vision got closer as if he was moving a few steps towards the back of the class where Victor was seated.

I didn't mention it or abruptly turn around in order to avoid looking perturbed in full view of potential questioning students. My attention was swayed even as I had begun writing and was actively in a middle of a lesson. With my eyes and nose facing the board, whiteboard marker in hand I paused as I absorbed this vision of the elderly, slightly rotund and affectionate white-haired gentleman who seemed to be here for a specific reason.

On my 'other channel', the vision in my mind, I was now being shown a lengthy, tropical back garden which led down to an embankment of thick, lush-looking reeds overlooking a swampy river. It was indeed vivid. I couldn't quite see the river because of the long, thick water-reeds but I knew it was right by his home. It was just like being shown a video with some of the shots frozen. It was photographic and iridescent in its vivacity and clarity. What photos enable you to taste, feel and touch in a variety of multi-sensual ways? If you see a swamp in a photo can you always smell the pungent odour of the wet soil?

But suddenly it changed, it wasn't a pleasant image I was now being shown. Still with my marker to the whiteboard to demonstrate a grammar point, I was being shown an enormous thick-bodied, tropical python-looking snake. It was ominously creeping up the garden path out of the riverbank and into a wooden house on stilts. After the lesson had finished, I asked to speak with Victor. Most students introduce themselves or certainly make their presence known in one way or another, but Victor hadn't said a word in class up to this moment.

As I asked him to verify who and what I saw, the look on Victor's face as he listened to me was one of speechlessness. He listened with trepidation and eagerness for me to finish the rest of my descriptions of his small home village and infamous snake event, which had indeed been a troubling experience for everyone. His jaw quite literally dropped, which I will never forget. He went on to describe and confirm how the huge snake had come into local houses and had also killed at least one child in the village. The snake was eventually spotted by the grandfather in the garden creeping and manoeuvring its bulky body out of the swampy, long garden reeds – and the grandfather had indeed been wearing the blue overalls at the time.

As far as my senses could make out, he had already passed over and was now watching over his grandson who was far from his native home in an unfamiliar country and very different surroundings. I have no other explanation why I should 'see' what appeared to be his grandfather standing there as clear as a fresh photograph. I assume he was giving the best identifiable evidence he could to share an experience that Victor would recognise as being only known by someone close to him, and that being his grandfather.

During class that day I had asked a group of students including Victor to come to the whiteboard to complete an exercise. What ensued was indeed bizarre. Following lunch break, but now with a different class for the afternoon period, my attention was drawn to an object between my chair and directly under my desk. What's this? I thought. I knelt down to inspect it closer and realised it was an antiquated-looking silver and wooden crucifix. The students could see the surprised look on my face.

I picked it up and immediately *knew* it must belong to Victor despite the fact that I was sure he had not been wearing it. I excused myself briefly from the classroom leaving a responsible student to mind the rest of the class, hurried next door, knocked on the door of the lesson in progress, entered with permission and spotted him. I held up the crucifix and said to Victor – "is this yours?" The look on his face was another one of shock as he stared wide-eyed at me, with jaw dropped open – a totally astonished expression, gratefully taking back the crucifix. It had belonged to his grandfather and according to Victor it should have been in the house where he was lodging in East Timor and neither around his neck on that day or at the school! I have no explanation for this.

I have heard of cases of teleportation and materialisation of objects from one dimension to another although I am not indicating this here but neither ruling it out. Can we connect this crucifix phenomenon with the appearance of his grandfather? I think we can. You may reach your own conclusion, but I have to say that in my time, I have come across some rather unusual occurrences and they have been witnessed by friends and colleagues – in this case by a student. I am sure he will not forget that experience either and neither have I.

Victor avoided me after this event. I never discussed it again either. I get different reactions from all sorts of people on the receiving end of these kinds of experiences. Needless to say, I also learnt from this lesson.

Unpleasant events of fear or even death and tragedy can also unexpectedly be relayed clairvoyantly. This may have been the last time the contact here in the physical world was with their loved ones, so the spirit was using the rare opportunity to convey and identify who they are. In this case, a crucifix, a memorable and haunting snake event that only the recipient could have known along with his grandfather's shared experience. I know that some mediums hear a voice whilst others see a person but most like myself, sense or usually are shown the spirit of the departed. However, we may not always be given a good look at their facial features close-up and also not always realise they have passed over. With the right training however, this should be overcome and therefore improved.

Chapter 11

Manila and Beyond

I have visited The Philippines a few times, but wrote this account three years before the horrific tragedy of Typhoon Haiyan in 2013. There is no connection here to that specific period.

I was soon able to realise that I had the capacity to sense spiritual vibes on my travels and one particular country where I feel vibrant, productive spiritual links is in The Philippines. I have found most of Filipino people very accepting of spiritual communications despite fervent Catholicism being a dominant part of their lives. But then, that ironically probably helps too. The devotion to the Holy Spirit and the ambience of the blessed statues of Angels and the Virgin Mary can be quite moving. I certainly got a little emotional walking around the ancient Basilica in Cebu and the Sunday service packed with families was incredible. Here, this ancient building still has the remnants of the giant crucifix, which was placed by Magellan, the Spanish explorer who is believed to have visited around the year 1521.

I had stayed in Manila for a few days and then headed down to Mindanao, a province further south. I caught a ferry to a remote island assisted by a friend. From the harbour port you can see a statue of The Virgin Mary directly in front of you on the adjacent island. I had expected to explore an island similar to those in the Maldives – sun drenched, with palms and long golden stretches of soft sand, which they tend to have more abundantly in and around the Island of Boracay. To my delight, this particular island was surrounded with thick, lush greenery set on volcanic rock and well-inhabited as well as some soft white sand and volcanic pebbled beach. I heard even the former President Arroyo used to drop in there to see how her 'project' was going on. Well, at least I could see this in the public relations poster at that time, which was still on display. I managed to get escorted and shown around the island by a young friend, Angelito who I had previously given brief readings whilst on a visit to the wonderful Basilica Cathedral in Cebu.

At that time I had met him in the hall of the Basilica with his head in his hands, after failing his law examinations for which his family had high hopes with all the pressures that accompanied it. It was here that we struck up a conversation which led to an eventual, cordial invitation to his parent's home on this quaint island to meet his girlfriend and family, who were waiting at the other end for us at the ferry port. We needed a four-wheel drive vehicle here for sure and luckily they had one. On the island I was eager to visit the local church. I seem to be drawn to Catholic churches, as some of them can be so colourful, which exude an angelic ambience especially with the Holy statues adding to the spiritual effect.

On discovering a little church nestled amongst the lush, vegetation at the end of a palm-leafed lane, it was so picturesque with the statues in bright, glowing whiteness emanating a kind of heavenly aura. I approached the cavernous, arched entrance and old wooden doors firmly fixed with a sturdy heavy-looking crucifix. This attracted me like a bee to pollen on a bright flower. The atmosphere inside was warm and an early evening service had just begun, with an accompanying small choir. They were singing in what seemed to be a total harmonious key and it felt angelic. This echoed out through the doorway as we were approaching and it was quite a refreshing scene after the bumpy bus journey and ferry crossing. The atmosphere now felt so uplifting and serene. Yet again, I seemed to have arrived at the right time.

I was greeted by a small group of mixed-age locals who were courteous and interested in saying hello to this new foreign visitor. Being the only Caucasian among the crowd at that particular time and as a stranger, I was more easily noticeable as a new guy in the village. It seemed most people on this part of the island knew each other. I was approached enthusiastically by one curious, friendly young woman with a wide smile, short and bespectacled. As she greeted me, I suddenly felt spiritual contact. I should add this doesn't happen all the time but it did here. I promptly asked 'who Jennifer was?' as this name came straight to me.

She let out a little high-pitched squeal. Jennifer was so excited by the fact that I got her name without telling me what it was. I was pleased, grateful but a little surprised to have this person's name 'given' to me on this occasion and in timely fashion. It must have something to do with the church we were standing outside I thought, as the small but impressive choir continued singing their harmonious vocals.

Just at that moment, I was then able to confirm with her that I felt that she was currently taking care of someone who had a disability, couldn't walk and whose legs had a special medical condition. It was clear she had been doing her best to care but it wasn't working out as well as it should. I was able to mention that she was being watched for her good deeds and that her deceased grandmother was around to see her doing it. Jennifer began to cry softly, her voice changing with emotion, with water-filled eyes confirming she had just recently been caring for a sick child who did indeed have the symptoms I had described. It was obvious she cared so much for the disability of the child. Of course there were other personal details here, and by now slightly embarrassed, I had already gathered a small crowd around me, which had been standing around the doorway listening to the choir. I wasn't used to this, that's for sure.

One friendly-looking, portly, middle-aged man with chubby cheeks who seemed to be hanging around eavesdropping intrigued, approached me and showed all the mannerisms of needing to chat. I seemed to be picking up almost immediately some important situations in his life so I knew I had to go for it there and then. I was on a roll with that psychic buzz and link again. After all, I'm an opportunist in more ways than one, spontaneously of course.

A sudden vision began to develop again as I focused with meditative concentration. I told him that in his life, I was sensing a lot of religious books around, whilst seeing him stand at an altar. He confirmed the reason for this and proved to be part of his actual occupation in involving missionary work. A stream of names concerning close friends and family for identification purposes began flooding in. However, I suddenly felt that I may now be treading on eggshells – metaphorically speaking, of course.

At this point I gently asked him if he was emotionally ready for a personal message containing rather private and delicate details and if he wished for the rest of the lingering small crowd of friends and churchgoers to be present. The rest of the group moved away politely which included one little boy who was sat on a basketball and staring right at us intrigued, as he watched and listened with curiosity. He was resting his head in his hands trying to hear whatever he could in an inquisitive way with that innocent look that only children can show when their attention is held.

Meanwhile, I could feel that there was something quite burdensome about the man's life, which he struggled with whilst working in the community and living his personal, daily life. For a moment I was feeling like a psychic counsellor rather than an off-duty teacher.

'Your mother says that it's ok to be <u>who</u> you are and not to let it bother you like it has done for so long – to just be a good person and carry on with the adoption although it won't be easy'.

Did I just say that? I thought. Well that was exactly what came to me at that moment as I paused again for anything else I could possibly pick up. It felt right to say it and I felt an emotional and caring, spiritual influence to do so at this particular time.

When I had finished there was a tear in his eye as he firmly grabbed my wrist and astounded me by saying "Thank you so much! You have made my life more complete". Gosh, I thought, I didn't expect that kind of response. I got so much out of hearing those words, felt humbled and thanked god and spirit for it is rare to hear glowing compliments from someone including a stranger. It made me also feel that more gratified hearing I had actually been able to help. And all of this outside a quaint little church with poor street lighting in the tropics. I had only planned to walk in and view the church and listen to the sweet harmonious tones of the choir. I could be forgiven for thinking that I was not only a teacher anymore. But the accrued counselling and tutorials I had given students over the years had always been beneficial.

Later on, avoiding potholes in one of the few worn out and weathered roads in a rickety old Jeep, I left the island by ferry for my final stopover in Manila. I went out for a meal at The Green Belt complex in the centre of the city. This is a modern dining and shopping area for what appears to me to be for tourists, business and wealthier visitors. As I sat waiting for my vegetarian pasta meal I picked up the spirit presence of a girl about the age of four or five around the young restaurant manager who was also attending as the waiter. I was also sure he only had one child. I decided to call him over to my table in a discrete way. However, since the restaurant was virtually empty of customers at this time it seemed less intrusive. I mentioned to the young manager what I had just felt and whether he had children. Mr Ramirez confirmed he was the father of young girl age five exactly. I asked him if he could explain what the 'water' around his daughter was. He said his daughter is constantly attracted to water and that he had taken her there recently to play. Well, nothing so surprising there, I thought. Most children love to be near the water. I pondered this. I felt that there must be a good reason to mention the obvious and gently indicated to him in an advisory way to teach the daughter to swim as soon as he could. In situations like this when we pick up images and words – it is hard to exactly know what the issue is, and in this case about 'water'. I felt the need to ask for more information to my spirit guide within a split second whilst simultaneously being the receiver of information and any form of message. It is similar to teaching in the sense that whilst focussing on the class, the other psychic channel is buzzing away and alert, never dormant.

As I saw his child in my mind's eye I believed there could be a future possibility of trouble. So naturally the best thing was to advise him to teach the kid to swim as soon as he could and not to worry her too much. However, I often pick up on achievements and disabilities such as someone who cannot swim – or the other way around if they have won awards and are quite skilfully adept at their chosen sport or craft. This was the case with a Korean girl in my class, as I was writing on the whiteboard (seemed to be the most popular time for my psychic adrenalin) I saw a violin around her and could even hear it.

Being a musician myself, it helps. She confirmed she did indeed play the violin and was the only one in the class that did. However, for the young manager here in the restaurant, I sensed something else, – the point where we feel there is a sensitive and personal issue involved that has to be handled delicately. I discreetly asked him if I may say something highly personal and of a sensitive nature, which he obligingly agreed as I was drawn to the womb and saw a foetus issue.

He told me his wife had had a miscarriage around six years ago and sadly lost the baby. For me personally, I believe that the girl who was now age five was probably from the spirit of the previous unborn baby from the miscarriage. Therefore, there was not a loss, spiritually speaking. This again was the *knowing* feeling as described before. I went on to confirm with the young man that he really didn't like his job, wanted to move and would do so around two years from now. He confirmed he had been there for five years and was seriously thinking of moving job, home and career and really wasn't happy with it.

I felt that the restaurant manager was being watched by a guardian in spirit, who was with him and knew about his situation and so therefore was being guided. Small comfort when you are trying to muster up as many Philippine Pesos as you can to survive, yet this is what I felt and it was all I could do to light up his path. I can't keep in touch with everybody although it would be nice to know the eventual results of some of those communications I have done on my travels.

In another part of Manila in Makati downtown area I was walking through a rather run-down shopping complex wandering through the various departments looking for nothing in particular. I was really avoiding the child beggars who I had been hassled by a few times and was advised may be part of organized gangs in the vicinity and therefore not all of them being genuine. As I brushed past one young man in a white coat on the pharmacy counter who introduced himself as Reynaldo I almost immediately began to get names, lots of them, actually stacks of them relevant to him, in fact so many were correct on this occasion that I had to ask him if it were really true. But I have to say at that moment, it was only names. I introduced myself explaining what I sometimes do regarding spontaneous 'readings' and asked if I may confirm if he knew the string of people including one close friend, who I shall not forget called 'Romeo' – but no, there was no Juliet!

As I was mentioning one by one, without a 'maybe', or a 'possibly' each one did actually belong in his social circle. He was surprised as I was but not shocked as he continued to write down the stock-check figures in the accounts book across the counter so not as to neglect his duties. He was more intrigued at wanting to know why and how I knew, for which I had no answer. Even as I had left Reynaldo and went across the road to find a bite to eat, I got a vision again and an 'Andrew and the rope that snapped across the river'.

I had only left the shop five minutes ago and I was still sensing a message of some sorts. As I came back and approached Reynaldo, he smiled and said that was exactly who he was with when he was playing as a kid across the river. This ensued with a variety of images and situations within his life being conveyed to me and the fact that he would soon go overseas. He later told me he had just completed his nursing qualifications and so that overseas employment was now tentatively active on his mind.

In fact, I mentioned there was a spirit of his Grandmother watching, if not guiding him and passing on the information. Of course, some may say, 'well, surely she has been reincarnated by now?' I take that point too, but then there are those who say all family members that we knew when we were alive will be able to meet again before they themselves can move on to a new physical life. Don't ask me how that works out but there are many theories and opinions on this topic as we know.

As for the pharmacist, I was so convinced of his future outcome that for inspiration I went up onto the adjoining floor to purchase in mint-condition, from the second-hand book store, a recent edition of *'Travel to Europe'* guide book in glorious full colour! I handed that across the counter to him and said, 'here is a gift, something from the spiritual with a message of inspiration that you can and <u>will</u> achieve a job overseas and with effort and perseverance, this is your hope'.

Isn't it comforting to leave someone feeling optimistic and that they have been touched from spirit with evidence to prove?

I have been quizzed whether I can see the future and my response is a reluctant and cautious 'yes' but only to a degree. Well, that just isn't good enough you may respond and I can understand that! But mediumship and psychic work is not the same field totally. For myself, and this may differ from other psychics and mediums, I get a sense of some potential change in a direction of the person's life in one form or another. For example, when I met my cousin's daughter last year, I felt that she was going to be suitable with therapy or as a therapist in about three years' time. I was not aware at that time that she had just chosen a specialist course at university in that very subject. Therefore, being able to tap into the vibrations of a person's lifeline but not being able to specifically say the exact name of the eventual job that she would land is sometimes as close as it can be to 'seeing' the future for some of us.

Seeing or feeling the future – that is the question! I was once asked to do a reading for one of my former Mongolian students. However, at that time it was a rare, online reading, which unbeknown to me was really for his girlfriend. I hadn't known she was sitting right next to him at the time. In effect, she was testing me, which I am not usually keen on and neither is spirit in my view. I was only shown a photo and told to tell him anything about what I could sense from her. I had encountered this form of psychic viewing in group work training at College in London so thought I would give it a try again. If I had known that it was really his girlfriend that was testing me I probably wouldn't have agreed to it.

At the end of the half hour reading she prompted him to ask me about her future. I never feel totally comfortable about the 'future' question and not forgetting up to this time I had always considered myself a teacher in a classroom rather than a psychic with mediumship abilities. I was able to sense his girlfriend doing a psychology course in the near future but they both affirmed it as 'incorrect' but later clarified that she was intending to complete a counselling course. Well, how correct do people expect the information to be? I ask you! The subject of counselling involves psychology as an inter-related subject in my view.

I know that I have certainly dreamt about the future like most of us, more than I have otherwise been consciously able to remember and that includes my parent's car accident. But the accident happened two weeks or so later. Could I have prevented it? – that's another question.

Chapter 12

Tsunami

This brings me to an unusual feeling and experience I had whilst both in Thailand and subsequently, Sri-Lanka. I believe both were connected to that feeling and no doubt, others had them too – and this was the Tsunami. It wasn't my intention to leave Thailand at the end of November 2004. After all, I had plenty of time as I was now between jobs for which I had saved up enough money for at least another two months staying at budget lodgings.

Whilst in the process of arranging a ticket from Bangkok airport to Phuket, a popular island in the south of Thailand, I suddenly began to feel negative and rather tentative about heading there. It was a place where I certainly wasn't unhappy visiting normally. I had visited there a few times previously and had met friends who had moved or worked there at that time. Why this sudden change of mood? After all, I had planned a long stay on the palm-tree lined, sandy Patong beach to relax and take time what to do next with my life after one particular arduous, year of teaching.

Standing at the airport in front of the domestic ticket counter I decided uncharacteristically to pack up and return home to the UK. I had no commitments to do so, so it was an unusual decision. As my flight was via Sri Lanka this meant I had a stopover in Colombo, the capital city. Sri Lanka is situated at the bottom of the subcontinent of India, for those who may not be aware. It has been called the teardrop of India because of its location and tear shape also known as the Pearl of the Indian Ocean. It was in my hotel here that I began to feel vibes of something unpleasant looming, but on a deeper level. I wondered what was nagging at my subliminal mind just immediately on arriving. I felt for one moment, there was something uncomfortable about the area of my hotel despite its tropical beauty directly on the coast with a wide-open beach and panoramic view.

On arrival at the resort hotel and immediately after checking in, the elderly male room attendant who insisted on carrying my bags waved me to follow. We seemed to be going down a level of small stairs in a narrow, dark corridor instead of up a level and therefore no lift was needed in this case. As I followed him zigzagging along this narrow corridor we descended a further small flight of steps to what appeared to be into a musty-smelling basement suite, I began to feel strange –just *strange*.

Now a clearer vision began to develop as I was now visualising myself distinctively wading through murky water of floating debris and darkness. All of this was in slow motion inside the building towards the lower level rooms. These rooms, it so happened, were facing the seafront arena with large double patio-door windows in each room, rather like chalet style. In fact, opening these windows and you would be standing parallel to the beach with only a few rocks. Palm trees were swaying in a soft breeze and sea birds could be heard. Whilst I was following the room attendant to my room, I forgot him briefly. I was on autopilot in a kind of blurry-haze and trying to follow the flow of a channel rather like a longer déjà vu.

By the time I got to my room it felt even stronger – like water rapidly gushing in. I didn't feel comfortable at all in that room all night and I woke at 3:30 am, switched on the adjacent bedside lamp. Now the feeling was at its strongest and most resonant. I had this uneasy feeling that the ocean was going to suddenly pour in. I pulled the curtain, took a good look out the bay window and as the beach was on ground level could just hear the sounds of the waves as normal. Nothing peculiar was going on outside the beach view windows, as I closed the curtain. So why couldn't I sleep?

Nothing out of the ordinary was happening outside and I then thought to myself that perhaps it was just an irrational fear of water coming in. However, my 'irrational' fear continued to bug me throughout the rest of the night and right through to morning but I shrugged it off as just something uncomfortable and possibly my imagination playing up for which I had no reasonable explanation.

In the morning, I sat on the garden patio, which was surrounded by a wide, flat lawn with a splendid view of the ocean. I had an extremely early breakfast and in preparation for the taxi back to the airport. The breakfast was served directly on the beach by the breakfast chef with his tall, white hat and attentive waiting staff in their black and whites in front of the hotel. I gazed across the vast ocean which was tranquil enough and it didn't seem ominous. The sea was only a sandal walk away and the ground was as flat and turfed like a golf-course or bowling green with lush, palm trees swaying in a gentle breeze amongst pockets of windswept sand.

Within two weeks of arriving back in the UK the tragic and shocking news unfolded in front of all of us on the TV. Broadcast around the world, a colossal Tsunami had hit the peninsula from Indonesia right up to India and beyond swallowing coastlines along the way. It wasn't until much later after I had stumbled across a government statistical report. This stated official loss of lives and extent of damage that I discovered included a list of hotels that had either been hit badly or worse, disappeared altogether. My hotel had indeed been one of those on the list in Sri-Lanka and also Patong, Thailand was struck terribly. All of this has been such an enormous tragedy for those involved, a great loss and to this day the families and survivors can never get over it.

Whilst teaching in Singapore, one of the mature international students from Thailand on his first day, sat at the front near my desk. Just as I was ready to begin I sensed something negative that had affected him and I believed it involved Phuket, which is a major tourist resort in the South of Thailand. I felt spirit energy of several people around him and right there besides him for which the image of Phuket was most prominent before me. I often, like students to introduce themselves on their first day. As he was also from Thailand, I intentionally quizzed him if he had a specific, close connection to Phuket as an icebreaker. His eyes suddenly lit up as he told me he was there on that day of the disaster trying to rescue as many survivors he could with his bare hands. He paused and looked melancholic now as he described how many were his friends who lost their lives.

Since it was not appropriate for me to continue the topic and a spiritual reading within the classroom I refrained and continued the lesson as normal. However, it does demonstrate to me that we still hold energies intact in a memory system and that spirit is able to bring forward and highlight. In this case, most likely wanted him to know they were still there. The alternative is to accept that it was psychic phenomena within the aura's range, but then there was a strong emotional bond for which I believe it was of a spiritual nature as well.

Chapter 13

On the Road in, Rangoon, Burma (Yangon, Myanmar)

These negative energies seem to still leave an indelible presence. On a side trip to Burma otherwise known as Myanmar and a brief teaching event in 20014, I was visiting a former teaching colleague, Kyaw Aung and his parents in the former capitol city Yangon formerly known as Rangoon. His parents were distinguished professors of science and so I was well informed regarding local information. However, I did get the chance to meander around the backstreets. Being met at the airport in a strange country makes one feel at ease and I was fortunate.

The city of Yangon/Rangoon has little changed since the British left in 1948 leaving the remnants of its architecture behind although there is a new modern shopping development now in place. The rest felt as if I had arrived in a different time zone. It was still charming with its leafy boulevards and archaic, deteriorating, but still intriguing-looking buildings. As I walked trying to negotiate my way through vendors displaying everything from fruit to hot samosas, I avoided the precarious potholes of decades of neglect but this added to its character. Having said this, I wouldn't want to fall down one at night, during one of the frequent power cuts. Yes, there were power cuts, which occurred at almost any time of the day but I suppose it adds to the character of the city depending on how you view an adventure. Having said that, I had a nasty experience in a hotel lift late at night when the power was cut, leaving me fumbling around in the total darkness in a small steel tube with no air-conditioner, so that wasn't very pleasant. This decadence still remains from years gone by, and in many parts, untouched since the Second World War – just mind those pot-holes or you may break your ankle in the darkness of an unexpected power-cut! I do hear they are improving on this power issue though. Still, with its old-world charm and former British, colonial-era buildings there is much to experience. This was despite the economic hardship at the time of writing, due to the political situation and suppressed decay of its infrastructure but it is improving now and investment is coming in.

There are train lines, which will take you around especially from Rangoon to Mandalay. By train however, it could be more than a month's salary for an average hard working local, depending on what they are earning. Still, I wasn't here specifically for tourism. For my first visit I was here to meet some educated, humble friends but it wasn't long before I was picking up vibes as I walked past local vendors and even fortune tellers in the dimly lit streets. There is so much going on as they sit along the paths selling their wares.

On my first trip I had the invitation and opportunity to meet friends for whom I also believe the situation was spiritually linked. Often the mother of my former Burmese teaching colleague would say she and the family had undoubtedly met me in a previous life and were now back in touch with our soul's path. I felt flattered as she also mentored me on the Buddhist ways of life.

I will not forget the time as an eight-year-old I was fascinated – or I should say, fixated by a story in an old children's pictorial encyclopaedia of a Burmese family going about their daily life. It seemed so very different to mine but yet I felt an affinity with it. Yes, even at eight years old. I pondered what it was that made me freeze time by memorising the pictures from that little Burmese story so young.

After a visit to the Grand Pagoda in all its golden splendour I made my way to the only main department store at that time. After going through security scanners at the entrance I slowly entered the supermarket on the ground floor. As I began to meander around the aisles for nothing in particular, I soon felt what I could only describe as a truly overwhelming, negative, numbing sensation in my head. It was like wading through slow motion in a déjà vu. But now in my mind I saw and felt the horror of screaming people and the horrors of panic, destruction and carnage. I felt choking as if suffocating in grey-black clouds of smoke – in fact a myriad of all things that constituted terror. I was so affected by this sudden wave of feelings that I decided to get out immediately. I didn't get a chance to buy anything. I just knew I had to get out. Was this a premonition? I didn't know if it was something going to happen or just an irrational feeling but I had to get away. On the way back to my hotel, I passed military barracks with the usual ubiquitous government troops guarding the entrance chewing beetle nut, which gave them the appearance of black teeth. The walk took me about half an hour along a lengthy, leafy boulevard but I wanted to get back to my hotel after that unpleasant feeling in the supermarket.

When I arrived at my hotel room I quickly and eagerly called my Burmese friend's father, a distinguished Professor. I described the unpleasant experience and feelings that had happened at the department store and knowing about my 'sixth sense' as <u>he</u> called it, responded immediately without question in a matter of fact way he added, "I am not surprised. This was where the recent bombing occurred in the basement and many people died, Jonny". I suddenly thought, to myself. Oh my god. How could I have not realised it was here. This was the exact place that was shown to the world media a few months prior to my very first visit. (I have visited several times since) Sadly the perpetrators of that heinous crime were never caught.

Reflecting on that experience, maybe it was negative, lingering energies that I had picked up concerning all the pain and suffering. Perhaps it was not just a time bubble I had walked through and sensed but was actual spirit energy. Whatever it was, it was quite shocking and I cried inside for those that had lost their lives in such horrific suffering on such a day. I had just felt something of an unusual nature which I couldn't explain. One is brought closer to empathising with the sufferer this way even if they have passed over. It took me a while as an ordinary English language teacher to realise the gradual implications of being a sensitive with certain clairvoyant abilities.

These negative vibrations leave an indelible presence and this is one disadvantage of actually having tuned, clairvoyant abilities. That's just my opinion. As mentioned before, at times the feeling could be as if walking through deep water in slow motion with a ripple effect. It's not always advantageous and awe-inspiring to be 'in tune' in this way and there are those who say we can choose to switch off by closing down what we call, the chakras.

I will admit that with my observation, the average person is not lucky enough to own a decent car in Yangon or certainly not at the time when I paid a visit. I did say the 'average' and not the wealthier ones. However, from the airport I was now being driven to another township outside Dagon Central and accompanied with my Burmese former teaching colleague, his father and mother. Kyaw – pronounced in English as 'Jaw', was the teaching colleague whose class I had helped out with the 'little bit of magic' teaching at the International College. The car was relatively old but apparently, according to his father 'a reliable, sturdy friend that never let him down '... An old Japanese, trusty friend', he said. He certainly did love his car.

However, I suddenly felt the urge to ask him if he had a problem with the car breaking down recently. 'Oh no, no, Mr Jonny, this car is so reliable', Kyaw's father affirmed confidently and proudly as he carefully observed an oncoming, battered truck precariously negotiating the cavernous potholes. This was quite a skill to manage as we turned a sharp bend whilst trying to avoid crossing pedestrians and erratic bicycles and the odd rickshaw weaving precariously in and out. I felt prompted to ask him if his 'old Japanese, trusty friend' had a carburettor problem. Still giving me the same response, as the car was after all, his trusty friend and the engine purring smoothly as normal. Just at that moment there was a sudden shaking of the car as if struggling for gas to get through a pipe. The car shook like a choking animal as we jerked backwards and forwards simultaneously in our seats.

"Oh Mr Jonny, what have you done? This has never happened to me before!"

I was taken aback and rather embarrassed to be honest thinking it must have been an almost instant precognition! Minutes later, the car was able to somehow correct itself whilst the engine shudders and shakes stopped. It later on broke down for the first time in twenty years and had to be repaired on the side of the road by a mechanic. We all had our heads under the bonnet looking at the carburettor whilst being watched and harassed by a small group of street children for small change. We kindly tipped them for just leaving us alone, as we needed to get back on the road as soon as possible. Within fifteen minutes the car burst back into life and we paid the street mechanic for his much appreciated efforts and so we all got on our way. But it wasn't over yet.

Just as we were approaching a junction something unexpected happened. A car in front of us slammed on its brakes followed by a taxi, which had braked immediately behind, rear doors flung open from the force and impact. Out of the car door, stumbling onto the road, a mother and what appeared to be her young daughter thrown out sideward, sprawled flat out on the main road. It seemed like a nasty fall out of the car and impact. A few seconds later the child or mother could have been decapitated or something similarly horrific. However, the mother picked up her relatively unscathed daughter and the taxi driver drove off to continue their journey with the passengers as if nothing had happened. Well, it wasn't New York or London.

I saw a similar incident in another part of South East Asia. A pregnant mother who was balancing four kids on a motorbike with a dog in the front basket, a baby on her lap wearing only rubber sandals on her feet and a hefty bag of rice nestled between them. She fell off the bike at an intersection with baby still in her arms. A miracle I thought. They just brushed themselves down and got back on the bike after the accident. But this experience we had just witnessed looked like a slow motion movie or re-enactment of one – and all specifically made for us. Were we the participants of some kind of synchronisation or just innocent spectators of a coincidence?

The Professor thought otherwise and perhaps influenced me in this case to make me wonder too. Naturally, all of us in the car were horrified but relieved and The Professor repeated the same 'Oh, Mr Jonny, this has never happened before whilst driving for the last forty years!' I admit it was a bizarre sight. Well, don't look at me in that accusing manner, I thought. I did go on to say that perhaps it was going to happen anyway but if we had not arrived on the scene then it would have been curtains for the mother and the daughter who had fallen out of the car onto the main road. Perhaps one of the angels came to the rescue like an invisible Mother Teresa or Superman –was this synchronicity in all of its complex mysteries. Who knows? Would I leave Myanmar thinking "Oh no, Mr Jonny what have you done now?" Ok, well, a bit of an exaggeration for my assumed guilt but you get my meaning.

As mentioned in an earlier chapter, superstition is common in Asia and I certainly had enough occurrences to make my friends wonder. At my hotel on the Hill near the grand Pagoda I was able to sense what appeared to be the energies of an elderly man. I was already in conversation with the young assistant manager when I felt this presence, which I understood to be spirit.

Then the vision became a little more fluid and I was able to now describe his grandfather and what he did during his life. I know that some professional psychics are able to sense and identify actual spirit immediately but for me, and initially at the early stage in opening up, it was more about 'reading' information or seeing personal details rather than always seeing a spirits body or face. That came later or was spontaneous. However, I was experiencing real mediumship during teaching hours and on the street.

The next morning in my hotel an amusing situation was presented to me. I promptly came down for breakfast and went to the front desk to collect my breakfast coupon. Waiting in a row with smiles on their faces, three female reception staff holding their hands out, palms face up for a reading! I had to excuse myself out of that one and kindly reminding them I don't read palms or the future! I hadn't mentioned anything to the receptionists so I assume it got passed from the assistant manager. I try to be discrete where and when necessary.

Living in such a repressive environment I can understand and empathise that one really does feel the need to get a peep into the future. This is especially true when there isn't a lot of joy around on the horizon or a lot to look forward to, but then there is the cultural aspect here as well. Sometimes it is embarrassing when one can't deliver on demand. I am not sure that the reception staff on the front desk had understood what clairvoyance really was but then again I suppose I couldn't blame them. All I had done was tune into and relay some personal information about the deceased grandfather of the assistant manager and then passed it to the grandson who was working in the same hotel at the time. I certainly had felt a loving presence in the grandfather's spirit and as cliché as it may sound it was right to pass that on. I certainly can't say how long a spirit lingers around their families but we are often reminded by professional mediums that there is only the 'now' and time is not as we understand it to be in the spirit world, heaven or whatever you may like to call it.

It was now September 2014 and I was now back in Yangon/ Rangoon for the fourth time. I'd been offered a new teaching position and flew into Burma on a business visa arranged by the new school. I was a new member of staff here and I had hardly been introduced to any of the teachers except for a couple of rudimentary greetings. Only a few of the western staff seemed sociable and chirpy, with the rest morose and with their head in books preparing their next lesson. For a moment I thought I was back in The Middle East where life tends to be harder for most of the teachers. Anyhow, I needed some peace and quiet to plan my new class lessons as the staffroom had a severe lack of available seats and work desks. I headed off upstairs to the third floor and spotted an empty room, which I thought would be conducive enough to concentrate –classroom 3b.

I was wrong. It was instead it seemed, conducive for something else bizarre that I had never expected or prepared for. As I entered the recently freshly painted, unoccupied classroom it seemed all was ok. It was surprisingly complete with modern, school equipment and desks all neatly set in rows with a large, clean whiteboard. There was a small top window just enough to see into the corridor and a comfortable swivel chair for the teacher. I pulled the chair to sit and placed my books on an adjacent desk to prepare my evening's lesson for an outside corporate class.

I settled into the chair, relaxed myself and began meticulously going through my notes for the lesson ahead becoming quite focussed as I concentrated on the task. I needed a drink of water I thought, but changed my mind as I was on the third floor with a lift that didn't work and the drinking container was on the ground floor in the HR office. Yes, I was a bit out of the way here from the rest of the staff, assuming it to be nice and peaceful, I thought.

I paused to underline a note of my lesson plan with my ballpoint pen issued by the company. I hadn't been in the classroom for more than ten minutes when suddenly out of my focus behind and around me was a whack, bang, smack, crash!

The noise was quite deafening to me as I ducked to protect myself thinking the wall was caving in behind or a bookcase slamming head first towards me. As I now promptly swivelled in full circle on my office chair to inspect what the hell had occurred, I held my hand on my chest from the abrupt intrusion into my private space and time. What the heck was that? I paused in shock, as I now lifted up my feet from the floor to see if there was anything broken or any evidence. I then immediately looked around the room meticulously for any potential signs of damage or movement of objects. Everything seemed to be in place. So where had this vibration, immense and intimidating noise suddenly come from?

I left the classroom and swiftly made my way to the teacher's staffroom and slightly breathless from running back down the stairs, popped my head around the door to ask the other teaching staff if they had heard anything. Nobody had and everyone seemed much too busy with their heads in their own lesson preparation to be concerned. Besides, to them I was just a new teacher on the block regardless that I had actually 'been around the block' with over sixteen years' experience under my belt. But right now that was not relevant.

I politely asked one mature and portly, western teacher to kindly but quickly follow me back into the classroom to where it all happened. Examining the room he said swiftly "everything is ok in here" and I would be fine as nobody had reports of any odd occurrences. He left the classroom as quickly as he entered it before I could even ask anything, leaving me feeling a little embarrassed. Of course, it occurred it may just be something supernatural but I didn't want to jump to that conclusion just yet. I decided to brush it off as either a fluke or something.

Just as I was again settling back into my work, it abruptly happened again with the same crescendo around my personal air space. This was too much! This time I noticed the Director of Studies pass the classroom door window a few minutes after the second noisy intrusion and so I hurried outside into the corridor to catch him. I eagerly asked him to come into the classroom, which he obligingly did. By now there was total silence in the classroom and I was at risk of appearing strange which I wanted to avoid at all costs. I explained it all again and he acknowledged that it was indeed peculiar and "perhaps it is the speakers on the lap top". I thought that was a really unsatisfactory and rather flimsy explanation considering they were mini-speakers and not switched on anyhow. I quizzed him whether there had been any similar, unusual activity happening to other teachers, which he was not aware of despite it being newly built premises. There hadn't – up until this day that is.

He left to attend to some other business quickly downstairs. As I eliminated every possible natural cause I felt this experience was too significant to ignore, especially if it happened each time I was alone preparing my lessons. I was on my own with this I thought. I needed an answer or at least some other acknowledgement, as usually I am not one to be shaken at potential spirit and paranormal activity. I decided to hurry down the flights of stairs to the front reception desk. It was serviced by three Burmese, female staff looking rather unoccupied. One was trying unsuccessfully to cram staples into an empty stapler. There were a couple of students reading magazines at the very far end sitting on a couch waiting for their lessons. I wasn't familiar with the staff due to just joining the company and hesitantly, taking a breath, quizzed them if anyone had experienced anything of a ghostly phenomenon on the third floor in classroom 3b or even the entire school building.

Before I'd even had time to finish my question there was a gasp from all three. "The teacher has seen a ghost," they yelled. "Which room? What did it look like?" As I mentioned I hadn't yet seen anything but only heard with a crescendo of a mind numbing experience, I probed for more information about what was on the original grounds before the school was built. They immediately confirmed in unison that it had formerly been a local cemetery. I asked them again if they were really sure and all three were adamant. By now it was getting around the rest of the main office and I was wondering how this was going to be received by management. However, still reeling from the excitement of it all, I didn't remain in the building much longer there as I was posted mainly outside to corporate teaching, taught off-site.

But there was one important issue I had to do. I went back into the empty classroom 3b and self-consciously decided to speak to an empty classroom saying a little prayer of protection as I approached. I was in the vicinity of potential staff members although students hadn't arrived yet for their night-class, so I felt this discreet enough but had to be quick. As I stood alone in the classroom, watching the little window hoping that I wouldn't be spotted by staff or students, I said with a quiet but empathetic and compassionate, clear voice and in a respectful manner "You have made yourself well known and I now know you are here. There was no need to startle me. I ask you to follow the light, pass through to a new life and your family and friends will be there. Just follow it. It's ok to move on now" I expected another blast of noise and braced myself. There was a soothing calm as if I had just released some energy in turmoil from anguish. I never had that noisy experience again but then I decided to leave in a very short time anyway.

By the time this book goes to print I should already have visited the enchanting city of Mandalay – as well as met some other friendly, local people in the future, which I am sure I will. Having said this, it is difficult to assess if we are helping or hindering the recent situation that has engulfed the country for more than half a century. There is always hope.

Chapter 14
Pitfalls of Clairvoyance – Negative Experiences

Although it can be a blessed experience, the clairvoyance experience is not without its downside. As I have mentioned in my chapter *Singapore: A Spiritual Encounter*. Although there can be clear, positive results and effects it doesn't always end that way. I have been drawn spiritually to certain places, situations and people, occasionally giving a message, which often surprises the recipient and in a few circumstances render myself vulnerable. Although often there may not be any specific message it maybe just that spirit contacts just wish their loved ones to know they are still around, exist and are well. At other times we are given specific, detailed information which allows us some kind of remote viewing of a person's previous or past state of affairs only they specifically could have known.

For example, this may highlight areas of their lives where they have gone wrong in their life, is likely to head in a certain direction for which they were already planning or had the idea to do so. More often from my experience, it has been easier to sense the past and present predicaments, but can also in some cases shed light on future potentials that may manifest in their lives. And by now we should already realise that clairvoyance isn't really about fortune telling.

In one case in Singapore, I was running out of funds between jobs as I hadn't been working for a while. I had decided to move into temporary lodgings cheaply as possible in order to budget. It was here that the local owner and landlord, a stout Chinese man, who friendly at first began to take a gradual and distinct dislike to me. Initially it was all amicable and cordial. However, I began to see flash images of people who he had known and had 'business' dealings with. It hadn't been my intention to be able to identify the location of his friends in specific areas and the areas of travel he had been to.

I remember asking the landlord about his near death accident in New Zealand in which he almost drowned at that time. The shock of someone else knowing what he assumed as the impossible gave him goose pimples but left me more curious as why I should be sensing it in the first place! Needless to say, my welcome was soon outlived and I was pressured to leave prematurely. Wouldn't it be rewarding if we could specifically pinpoint who was passing on such potent information? And as some may say in the professional spiritual business, one should try to discover their spiritual guide – the spiritual guide that relays information and takes care of us. This of course, is easier said than done. There seem to be too many out there who claim to all have Red Indian Chiefs as their own spiritual guides. On the other hand, we would have to have someone to assist us spiritually as this ability cannot only be the medium's ability alone.

Unfortunately for me, I began to notice that the local, Chinese Landlord who spoke Singlish, (a local dialect of English and Singaporean English) was becoming distinctively uneasy with my company. It wasn't because he had never had a Western lodger before, despite the fact I was as impeccably polite, quiet as a mouse and spotlessly clean in habit.

My new, temporary landlord to my alarm was apparently a loan shark and now wanted me to move out much earlier than arranged. He told me his 'old friend' would be moving into the room next to me after fifteen years of being in jail for alleged attempted murder. This was a bit dubious as I assumed anyone with that charge never leaves a jail there. Everything was thrown at me for the emotional effect. I was getting jaded by the exaggerated stories of how he had used an AK47 with his mates on 'missions' overseas; of course all nonsense.

Whether I believed in it or not, that was not the point. "When are you leaving, lah?" in Singaporean-Chinese tonation, which was kind of direct in a suggestive manner. He was often getting goose pimples by my seemingly intrusive bits of personal information about his life, which in many cases he asked me for. "What you feel about me now, uh?" Well, I got the message pretty soon and decided to get out of that hell hole which was incidentally, chained and padlocked like Fort Knox for some suspicious, paranoid and over-protective reason. It was another good reason to leave bad energies behind. I had felt like a rabbit in a warren anyway.

One further, negative experience I describe here involves a threat towards me by a Thai manager of a bar. This I assumed was for unintentionally, revealing psychically some of his apparent shady but significant, recent past. This was despite the positive details I had mentioned about future potentials and developments on the horizon. All of this came from an on the spot mutually agreed, random, but intuitive reading without the use of angel cards. I had no prior knowledge of his life as I had just walked through the door and just ordered a cold beer. For obvious reasons, in this particular case, I cannot be too open with specific facts.

I sat in his bar in downtown Chiang Mai, in the north of Thailand. This was a place I have always enjoyed on many trips being attracted to its more peaceful setting. Chiang Mai, amongst other things is known for its hill-tribes, Trekking and traditional architectural influences. Over the years, I have stayed in hostels in guesthouses and many hotels of varying standards and these days impressive spa-hotels have cropped up in this area. I particularly love the wood art here and I have purchased a variety of their hand-made work over the years.

Once outside the hustle and bustle of its small, congested centre of mainly one-way traffic I would often venture way up to the Doi Sutep Mountain alone. The area is surrounded by lush vegetation and accessible by an almost never-ending winding and spiralling road. Once near the top I would often pay a visit to the temple or skip it depending on the number of tourists clambering out of the many parked coaches on their day-trips in their sun hats and shades. I prefer the quiet life.

I rented my own motorbike from the same garage for several years so developed a good friendship in a business manner. If I went to a bar I would sit and enjoy the evening and attempt the occasional psychic reading for one of the accepting bar staff or local – sometimes with great success at times if I was in tune.

I had never had a serious problem in my time spent in Thailand though I certainly have seen some very unpleasant occurrences too troubling to mention and came very close to it. However, if one is able to read the local Thai newspapers anyone can get a clearer view of what actually happens here. The photos can be quite graphic from all kinds of accidents to shootings in glorious colour and disturbing images. Privacy is not always a priority. The rules of being clairvoyant are not so tangible but there is a responsibility that one has to learn and practice if one is to venture into using a gift with the intention of helping others.

However, there was one situation which I came across and of which I learnt a lesson. I parked my motorbike outside a seemingly, inviting-looking bar and ordered a cold beer whilst listening to a local customer attempt karaoke. I was greeted by the manager and found a comfortable seat. The door was open to the street and a ginger-coloured cat was now strolling in from across the road as I sat facing the open doorway. It wandered to my feet, jumped up onto my lap and almost immediately fell asleep. It was almost as if the cat had gone into a trance. No seriously! It happened. I must admit I do like cats, particularly if they are friendly and affectionate and I even have a photo of one of my cats in spirit.

The young bar manager told me it didn't belong to him and it is not usual for a cat to wander outside in the street. He didn't seem to mind as long as I was buying his beer. As the evening moved on and I became the last customer I felt there was a need to do a quick reading for him. I asked him to politely sit down and mentioned my reason. As he agreed to the reading, I told him about how I felt a negative presence in his most recent relationship and that there was a business decision to be made particularly around the month of June. I felt a great deal of emotion in his life both past and present as if he feared or needed to hide something. He remained quiet and attentive but apparently unperturbed, which was misleading. I was able to continue in a discreet but constructive way about his predicament and emotional situation. It was those vibes again and you just go with the flow.

There was an issue which seemed negative and delicate but clairvoyantly ambiguous for which I couldn't quite define and mentioned it in an uncritical way. He barely mentioned a word as I carried on uninterrupted as he just acknowledged with curious affirmatives. He paused and nodded his head to my main points about his life and even wished me good evening as I left for the night as he pulled the shutters down. He said 'come again soon'.

Two days later I paid a visit to the same bar in the early evening. The manager was sitting at the table and chatting to his local customers and friends. He was handing them the ice bucket to go with their drinks and everything seemed jovial. However, as I walked to a seat and sat down on the wooden bench, ordered a beer from the waiter he stared at me with hostile intent as if the Lone Ranger had just walked in. He was now whispering something brazenly and ominously to his friends. He certainly wasn't smiling now. They were at this time drinking whisky but none appeared intoxicated whatsoever and also, as a group, were now staring at me in a very threatening manner. It was early evening and the bar has just opened.

At the same time, the same ginger cat across the road had again already wandered back into the bar plodded towards me, jumped up, sat on my lap and went back to sleep again. For some apparent, ominous reason, this hadn't passed their notice and the manager glared with ill intent as if preparing to throw insults or plot something. By now, I was distinctively feeling uncomfortable by these hostile glares and after only being in the bar for less than ten minutes I tried to finish my beer. I put on a false but uneasy smile leaving my unfinished drink and asked for the bill to which he now aggressively threw his hand out in front of my face and told me to pay and "get the f*** out of my bar and don't ever come back!".

The foul expletives were repeated for me and everyone in the street to hear. I left the bar promptly whilst gently dropping the cat to the floor. As I made my way swiftly to my rented motorbike the profanities were still echoing. The group were now shouting in unison outside the door and into the main street at me. Only the Rottweiler dog and a weapon were missing, as I had images of it ripping the back seat of my pants or savaging my leg. If it hadn't been so serious it would have been laughable. I hadn't come across such caustic hostility since the time I had walked into a bar in Grand Junction, Colorado, knocked the sugar bowl off the counter in a Hicksville-rockers bar and was deliberately and falsely accused of stealing 50 cents off the pool table all for no other reason than to cause trouble. The difference here in Thailand, being it specifically had something to do with my reading that sparked it in my opinion. Still, I got the message and certainly felt the intense, negative vibes. I drove back to my hotel visibly upset as I had never had the intention of offending anyone –and besides, my brief readings always came from the heart with the sole desire to assist in good faith. I usually display compassion and sensitivity.

I believe that we have the opportunity to change and influence the course of our own path. In a reading if I became aware that some difficulties may manifest in the future for that person, I would express it in a way that supported them to believe in their own abilities and overcome it should the problems arise. So in the case of this young Thai manager I am sure I focused on the positive aspects. It was the reality of a stranger 'knowing' about his dubious and secretive past he most likely was horrified about. This is where it sounded alarm bells in his mind and to me it was odd that he showed not one sign of it during the reading. This was I suspect, fear.

As I sat in my hotel room, I reflected on the previous visit to the bar and the original reading I had given but can only assume I may have unnerved him about a serious issue from his past which had remained a total secret to that day. Ironically, if anything, I believe I had become *the* threat and this is why I also learnt a hard lesson in not being too open about what is sensed on the day. It pays to leave things untouched on certain occasions and that was one of them.

A little later after this, I hadn't planned being stuck in the middle of a coup d'état but that's exactly what happened. It was 2014 and anti-government protesters were blocking major intersections and paralysing the city of Bangkok. My small, rented bungalow room was located on the opposite end of the mob of protesters down a long, meandering alley whilst at the other was a tuition centre I was assisting at.

I had to go through the noisy mob each day but on one occasion it was the busiest and rowdiest event on a weekend. It was jam-packed with people and I wanted to get home. Suddenly, I felt and saw in my mind an explosion and I sensed danger. I needed to get away from here immediately. I decided to run for possible safety but with difficulty due to the crowds blocking the way from all directions. As the megaphones were blasting across the area and people blowing their whistles at anything given chance, I kept on running until I was well away from the area, feeling vulnerable and unsafe.

Three days later, my early alarm call failed to wake me on time. I was now delayed by twenty-five minutes for school. As I briskly walked to the tuition centre where I was helping out part-time, I rather strangely seemed to get confused, losing my sense of direction. I had done this route many times and so could not figure out why. I suddenly noticed the intersection had gone silent and deserted. Police and ambulances were now hurrying in all directions to where the protesters had been gathered. I quickly soon discovered that a possible grenade or small explosion had gone off killing and also injuring bystanders. It happened in the exact location to where I had sensed something of danger, three days earlier. We all have a sixth sense and if only it proved to be as beneficial and in-tune for all of us as it had been for me at that time. I was just lucky. Twenty-five minutes earlier would have been a different matter.

On another occasion, I was working in a new job in the English Language department and the technical engineer was called in to repair the computer in the office. As he was going about his job I sensed some strong personal details of his life including his own feelings and emotions. I asked him to confirm that his little daughter had just begun school and that he was concerned about the funds for the new school term and her recent sickness as his wife and daughter were far away overseas.

I am not in this case saying this incident was passed from spirit but I was able to sense clear suppressed emotions for his family at that time for which he would certainly have been experiencing. I was being shown the name of his hometown and major city (Madras) in India and that it was right near the water. When the energy is on a 'buzz' as I prefer to describe it, then I follow the flow even if doing other tasks such as teaching in the classroom or working in the office. Now that has to be real multi-tasking! I am as equally moved as the recipient if the unexpected information is more exact. One just feels the need to pass it on as it comes. But it's not as if we have a personal diary of their life. We wouldn't know exactly if it may be true unless they confirm it and it's not as if we are going to go out of our way to investigate the facts later for proof. For me, I just relay what I receive and for the most part, with discretion and sensitivity.

In the computer engineer's case, he later questioned colleagues and staff if I had actually been accessing his personal information on the company's hard drive! As a matter of fact, I was teaching all day so there wouldn't have been the time to get access to personal information of this kind and to be honest I certainly wouldn't have any interest even if I could. As you can imagine this did get around the school office with quite far reaching and over-exaggerated negative responses. It was partly the reason for my resignation. The school department primarily consisted of a mixed bag of superstitious, multi-cultural Asian staff. Not all cultures and office politics react in the same way as in the West. Exaggerated and spiteful gossip spreads like the mumps although some can be sympathetic and intrigued. It's a lesson to be learnt but having this type of gift is not easy to suppress despite it being a part of our god given creativity.

I was once told by someone who said that if a psychic came up to them in the street and said something personal to them about their life they would want to punch them. Well, it exposes the insecurity of such a person in feeling that they do not have or cannot control what they consider as personal or intrusive. It's not as if a psychic would approach someone in the street and ask them to confirm if it really is true that they take Viagra on a regular basis and have been sleeping with their best friend's partner in front of their current partner! Now that *would* be unethical and an infringement on their personal life.

However, I have encountered stage mediums on stage and one I can recall was in a city theatre with a large audience. The medium mentioned to the receiver something very personal for all to hear claiming what the person in spirit had been doing together with them in their relationship. I found that private information being aired in public objectionable. I often wonder if spirit is aware in these public auditoriums that the link is being shared with potentially hundreds of strangers. This would make it similar to a mass conference telephone-chat call except it's usually a one-way channel. 'Mom says is Uncle Alf still wearing her underwear?' Kind of embarrassing example for the poor guy as the medium quite carelessly announces to a surprised audience. Meanwhile, the recipient of the message sinks into his seat a little deeper, red-faced. Or maybe that's an understatement.

Chapter 15

Pet Angels

Since writing this book and attending a well-known Spiritualist college in a beautiful Jacobean Mansion in Essex near London, I had begun to notice an increasing amount of orb and spirit photography, which often produced a variety of faces in my photographs. This included what appeared to look like my deceased dog and cat within the photographs. The photography could be quite detailed showing all the normal features such as eyes, ears, nose and mouth including teeth etc. I have always loved animals and this contributes to a close bond I have had whether they are wild or domestic. This probably explains why I am frequently able to unconsciously pick up information of pets in spirit or living from strangers fairly quickly and in most cases it was from my students.

Whether it is birds in the garden, hungry and abandoned cats in the street to friendly dogs or horses, I find them endearing as well as engaging to watch especially when they are lost, ignored or abandoned. Most of these trusty, companionable animals often seem to be able to identify instantaneously who has the benevolent touch regardless of whether or not one issues food to satisfy their hunger.

I still dearly miss our St Bernard dog, as he was a predominant part of the family life and particularly mine when we were living in the countryside. We had several cats that all treated him like their own giant sibling as they grew up with him playing with his floppy, soft ears and often taking a playful swipe at his tail whilst sitting on his back. I often wondered how our dog knew he would be going for a walk with me when I hadn't alerted him at all. This would occur immediately I had the thought to do it when we were in separate rooms and at totally opposite sides of the house. There was no set, regular walk time so that explanation was ruled-out.

Suddenly, the moment I had the thought to take him out for a walk there would be a rumbling down the corridor followed by a tremendous thud as the door crashed open, narrowly missing pot plants, as the rug skidded halfway across the hall. This was similar to a small horse when it comes to an abrupt halt in full flight – except it was in the house. This reminded me of the old Hollywood movie *'Beethoven'*. It involved a cumbersome but loveable St Bernard dog. I should say our dog walked me like a husky pulls a sled, as he was powerful enough.

In his last days of his life, about ten days before our St Bernard dog died, I had a vivid dream that I was in a telephone phone box in a country lane calling my father. Full of sombre emotion I clearly heard "Billy hasn't made it, Son. I'm really sorry, there was nothing we could do." I had emotionally told my parents that if they put him to sleep in the vet whilst I was away I would not return from my proposed European trip ever again. For a large dog, I have been told that the back legs often go first and therefore, as far as I understand it, their body-weight cannot be supported like it used to.

On return from my trip to Paris and Amsterdam ten days later, it was raining so I had to make a quick call to my father for a ride back home. It was then that I received the heart-breaking message that our dear St Bernard had died. I was in tears. He was the biggest teddy bear one could have ever wanted who took up our sofas when we weren't looking and left giant paw prints in the neighbours' freshly raked garden soil. He had now gone to his heaven, wherever that may be and his remains are now a big mound under an old oak tree.

Of course it is often the case in spiritual services that pets come through to the medium present. After they have passed it is possible that our pets appear in some form or another and these can, in my experience, be seen also in orbs of light on camera. Others may sense their deceased pets nearby and in some cases clairaudiently hear their cry or greeting, feel their weight sitting on the bed or around the vicinity they are in. This can be whilst we are either awake or half-awake. It may not be the case that the pet spirit is around the owner all the time but they seem to drop by either unexpectedly or when one is reminiscing about them. I know that when I have sensed a person in spirit they would often appear with a pet with them and that too would further identify the spirit being channelled to the sitter.

The fact is we can't prove this to the scientific researcher, but then it cannot be disproved either for people like myself and many others who experience it. We just know. Such was the bond with both my dog and cats that I have always felt this empathy with pets; these trusted friends of unconditional love and loyalty, which differ from many humans in that respect. However, I can't seem to warm to the idea of carnivorous animals of prey as I believe what they kill also has a right to live too.

The day before one of our much-loved cats died I had to get on a plane for Vietnam. My cat watched me pack my bags, followed me in the room and sat on my shoes looking up at me meowing constantly. She died in my father's arms the next day. Most likely, she knew she was going to pass away wanting me not to leave and give her the last hug. She had reached the ripe-old age of twenty, and lived a good age for a cat.

Despite thousands of miles in distance, working or travelling away from home, and absence at their deaths, I sensed that each pet had already passed over in one form or another. This often occurred in dreams or message thoughts. In one case, I was actually fully awake and conscious and witnessed what I believed to be one of our cats inside my room in spirit.

The only problem was, it was so real I thought at the time our cat was actually still alive. It was in the city of Bangkok Thailand. One morning I awoke for School and prepared to get ready for work. Anyone getting to this apartment would need a motorbike or risk twisting the ankles falling in sunken potholes with potentially lethal metal cables protruding erratically and precariously from walls and stone slabs.

As I was shaving one morning and standing directly in front of the mirror getting ready for college, I was drawn to the attention in the corner of my eye's peripheral vision. Here I was, on the 17th floor of a high-rise apartment block and I had just seen a quick swish of one of our family cats twirl around the room then disappear into thin air. I was so convinced I had seen our cat that I swiftly opened the locked apartment door to see if it had walked down the hall. Of course this was unrealistic being so high up in a towering building and it would have had to take the lift! In any case, there was no doubt that it was my cat from the UK.

On that same night after work I fell asleep and had quite a vivid dream. In the dream, Tommy our family cat was being nursed by my father, in his arms at the animal clinic, where he appeared to be sombre and unusually tearful. This was not something I had noticed him being in these situations. Two weeks later I went back to the UK and on enquiring where one of our cats was, discovered that he had indeed been taken to the vet. He had been nursed in my father's arms who had been visibly upset and tearful. This occurred on the same day, two weeks previously that he passed over where I had the vision of the cat in my room. Either he was saying goodbye or I was picking up emotional distress vibes – distance being no object of course in the spiritual realm.

I have read about other people's experiences regarding animals passing away but I have to say that where there seems to be an emotional bond there will be also a spiritual link. I am not the only one and there are many who have known this to be so. On a more positive note, away from home still in Thailand, I remember picking up the spirit of an owner's dog and the descriptive details as I was sitting at the side of a bar for an evening drink. Nok, the amicable coffee shop owner confirmed she did indeed have a small brown and white dog with its left ear dashed with a blob of white. ('Nok' means 'bird' in Thai.)

I do tend to sense owner's deceased pets and am sure others can too. And as mentioned before, the school classroom was a hive of activity regarding the students' pet vibrations – In spiritual terms it was sometimes like a menagerie or spirit zoo! All this as I was trying to write on the whiteboard, essential English vocabulary during a lesson.

I asked Nok, if she had buried her much loved family pet at the bottom of the garden under the tree when she was about five years old. When she was only five or six years old, she confirmed that the dog, named 'Guy' after it had passed away, they had actually placed it there when she was age six. A sudden tear welled up her eye as she confirmed and described how she loved that little dog so much. I said to her that I felt its spirit was still alive and is paying you a visit here by returning the love.

Stranger still was that just at that moment; a small dog walked into the shop off the main road, approached Nok first and gently held up its paw onto her knee. She was so struck by this and confessed she had never seen a dog do this to her – Certainly not in that neighbourhood. The dog looked at me with an amiable twinkle in its eyes, cheerfully wagged its tail once more and sauntered off into obscurity in one of the dark backstreets. I couldn't help thinking that spirit made an effort to influence a street dog to do that just at the exact moment in time we were tuning into the memory of her pet dog's passing and possibly its spirit.

Nok added that street dogs here just didn't act with that kind of behaviour as most of them would be too nervous unless they were treated well by any potential owners. I agreed with that after myself having a scary experience being pinned to a wall by a pack of nasty 'Soi' dogs at one o'clock in the morning. 'Soi' means 'street' in Thai Language. We actually saw it approaching with specific intent as it waddled in a direct manner through the tables and chairs to get to its recipient. It's not unheard of for spirit to influence an animal. It is also not unknown for spirit to influence someone in the physical world to sit up and listen; in this case it may have been the spirit of a dog or a deceased person affecting the animal's sense of direction. Well, it's not impossible.

Since writing this chapter and taking a break from teaching I resumed my spirit photography endeavours. I have been able to catch some interesting images, of not only cats, dogs and other animals, but spirit people as well. I was deeply moved after going through the photos taken in the backyard, which included a clear enough image of our St. Bernard. I felt prompted to put this small slide-show video on the YouTube website at the time as evidence. Since becoming involved in this phenomenon, some call 'orbs', I have been able to catch on camera as experiments, a diverse range of spirit activity in the form of ghosts and unusual images either transposed onto myself or onto objects.

For faces and images to appear of course, this would only be able to occur if there is intelligent communication taking place between the photographer and an entity. A very small sample of evidence of this can be seen in my photographs both in this book and on my website.

Chapter 16

In the Staffroom –Hungarian Spirits say Hello

Each of us has our own character, personality and energy and we have to be careful not to send out any unconscious negative impulses and thoughts. These can be picked up unconsciously and transmitted from and to each other in their 'air space' and range of our aura –even to strangers. We are in effect, human antennae. I am sure most of us have had the feeling that someone doesn't actually like us before we have even had the chance to become known to them. This is not always paranoia or simply by observing their physical mannerisms. But then also there are the positive vibes that permeate our mind and auras being transmitted from one to another unconsciously. This is regardless of whether one is a practicing psychic or not and that includes the skeptic. It's an ability we all possess and some that seem more comfortable to deny.

In the case of one amiable, energetic head teacher and colleague however, I could feel her energy immediately even though we were not yet acquainted. I am not aware that she felt my presence at all as I sat preparing my lesson plan discreetly behind my piled-high, precariously stacked class files. I do always focus on sending out positive thought impulses and you will be surprised how this can work if you are in spiritual thought and practicing it habitually.

So what was it that made me feel my new teaching colleague reminded me of one of the lively nuns from the movie the *Sister Act*? Well, this was Helen along with her Hungarian-Canadian upbringing. She exuded nervous energy like static electricity similar to knicker-elastic rubbing against a woollen sweater. Spiritually speaking, I felt there was something more to her presence. Of Hungarian-Canadian origins, I met her whilst working at an Education centre in Singapore where the teachers taught mainly mainland, Chinese students English and a plethora of other subjects.

When there is a psychic buzz around a person I usually try to approach them in a discreet way regarding spiritual matters. Well, that is what I like to think I do most of the time. Then the rest seems to fall into place by the sixth sense of spirit leading the way. But when I sat down with Helen in a restaurant and began to get unfamiliar, non-English names of people and places she immediately and excitedly confirmed them. These were not only Hungarian sounding words but also of Germanic origin and some specific to her former deceased family relatives from Hungary. This even included one of her former schoolteachers with an unusual and less common Eastern European name.

I had no former background knowledge of Hungarian names and at that time had no knowledge of Hungary itself, so this certainly proved an eye-opener for Helen and me. Fortunately, her understanding and acceptance of the afterlife no doubt made it easier. Besides, it saves the embarrassment of explaining to a skeptic how you came to get such personal information if it does occur.

Fortunately, Helen is not one of those and it helps to be around like-minded people with positive vibes. Occasionally, she would bring her son, Ryan along for dinner who at that time was still in school. Ryan was fascinated by all of this. In my opinion, it was Spirit that would also like to join in, contributing little pieces of further evidence of what Helen's son had actually been up to in the classroom a few days earlier for our ears to hear! Yes, it was capable of that too when I composed myself and tuned in. She couldn't possibly have known what her son had been doing in the classroom without her being informed by him. In this case she certainly hadn't known.

I always aim for the quiet, more secluded spots for private readings and cafés or restaurants with high-back partitions are my favourite, especially the earthy, wooden ones with slightly dimmed lighting. We edged our way through the hungry diners manoeuvring gracefully through, sat at the table and began eating our scrumptious Indian, pure Vegetarian buffet meal. It wasn't long before I had received a picture with symbolic message 'Tell him about the oranges'.

Oranges, I thought? The picture flashed into my mind for which I could sense and even taste the acidic fragrance of citrus and freshly squeezed orange peel being propelled across classroom desks. This form of sensing is known as clairgustance and clairsalience, which includes taste and touch.

I prompted Ryan, "What is the entertaining occurrence that recently happened with the oranges? Does this make any sense to you?" Before I had even finished the sentence his eyes lit up with a broad smile, which developed into an excitable chuckle –"Oh yah! That's right Mom, we had a fight in the classroom and we pelted each other with oranges! But it was all in good fun! Quite a mess too! We all had a great time when the teacher was out of the class during the lunch hour."

Now who else could have known this? Helen, on hearing her son proclaiming such an orange-pelting event and assuming him to have been working studiously at the time, turned swiftly to her son said, "Ryan, you never told me you did such things like this in the classroom? You are supposed to be studying hard!"

I often wondered if it was Helen's mother in spirit who was able to pass on such detailed information as it was often personal and connected to her side of the family which was presented to me and not her husband's. It was often the case that I drew a blank when trying to tune in for anything about her husband's life or side of the family. However, I do feel that those who may be cynical or even sceptical of spirit and psychic communication obviously make it harder for not only people like me but also for themselves. In my experience, 'blocking the mind' and not being open-minded enough can hinder a communication process. They may not intend, or be aware of any blocking process, as it is quite deep in their unconscious, safe and sound where it lies.

During the reading, I would see Helen's grandmother's house, the little sitting room with the old cuckoo clock with a chip in it and see her entering the palatial grandeur of the Basilica church. What a wondrous site, being shown such a colourful awe-inspiring and decorative artwork of that grand dome and glorious, ceiling cupola! Helen confirmed to me she had indeed been into the Basilica to view such architecture and historical paintings which adorned the entire inner-roof. I was so struck with the visual image in my mind that this kind of clairvoyance might be termed as 'remote viewing'.

It was the day that really made us sit up with excitement and what better way to have an unexpected psychic link over a sumptuous, Indian vegetarian curry. Munching on our shared dish of pakora and chapattis in a curry of dal makhani I suddenly paused to say, 'I am getting an unusual name and it doesn't sound English. I am sure it is male and in the family'.

I clearly spelt out L-A-S-Z-L-O'. I grabbed a piece of paper and now was able to write the Hungarian accent above the vowel. Helen beamed with delight. She was evidently quite moved because this according to Helen was her deceased Uncle Laszlo from Budapest in Hungary. He had already passed over and I was now quite clearly being shown something quite special from her childhood that nobody else could have known except her. Even her son didn't know this and so it was for all three of us, a truly exhilarating experience. It's one thing to get it right confirming native English names from spirit but quite something when it's totally foreign. I surprised myself on that occasion.

I was now given more information sensing there was a stocky lady showing herself who was very good at playing a musical instrument, and a name sounding like 'Schumacher'. There was another chuckle of surprise as I was describing her old music teacher who had passed away long ago. Most of these characters from the spirit world seemed to be close friends of her mother's. That also, should have been the clue. There was no specific message here from Ms Schumacher, which led me to believe that at first I may have been picking up information from Helen in a psychic way rather than spiritual. I never rule that possibility out either.

However, as mentioned before, one cannot always be certain that it is not spirits making contact. After all, if it was her mother then she would be able to pass on specific information about each person who had been present in their lives –whether that is family, school or work –her mother would know. As with names there are also sounds being sensed which can be either auditory or clairvoyantly. But in my experience as I have developed, I prefer to describe it as 'psychic phonics' from beyond. The difference being it usually comes from within rather than outside the normal auditory reception.

I remember as a schoolboy reading from the famous medium Doris Stokes book *'More Voices in my ear'*, which greatly inspired me and she was someone who I admired. At that time as a child, I had assumed the words the medium 'heard' were interpreted to be just like a real voice.

Becoming a vessel and channel from the other side we have to learn how to interpret signs as well as translate words, which at times can sound like someone with pillows muffling the vocal chords. For example, 'Harry' may sound like 'Larry' but it should usually be close enough. Some never even sense names and describe the person in spirit leaving it for the bereaved to identify the clues. I mean what did you say – Larry or Harry? No, it's gone – lost forever. Often there isn't a second chance of getting it right either, especially if you have an audience, whatever size.

Although I began as an English Language teacher it was outside the classroom and on my travels that more opportunities arose to be able to develop psychic and spiritual links. I believe my experience in some situations *is* actually remote viewing and does not necessarily always imply there is spiritual help. However, occasionally, the quality and clarity of clairvoyant phenomena can also indicate it being from spirit. This is not contradictory but just a reminder that there are other possibilities at work when using psychic faculties and relaying information.

Naturally, not all people on the receiving end of a 'reading' react in the same welcoming manner as Helen. I have met a variety of people with differing opinions and attitude towards psychic and spiritual workers; those that are downright scathing or hostile, cynical or sceptical right through to the open-minded, fascinated and enthusiastic believer. The hostile ones seem similar to days gone by where it was forbidden to have any unusual ability and as a result was reacted upon with a vengeance and negativity. This would be regardless of whether the psychic unveiled correct information or not.

It pays to get the spiritual information as accurate as is possible. But I find it is often with trial and error as one just can't always be so sure it is actually correct unless the sitter finally confirms it from their own memory or own honesty. They can and do actually forget significant pieces of past experiences themselves. Then there are cases when seeing potential future events makes it even more of a task for the clairvoyant. Sensing the time aspect inaccurately can therefore risk further criticism.

You may then say, then why bother? Well in my case, if I hadn't then I wouldn't have been able to have written about this subject regarding just a few of my personal experiences. If something works and produces results for a recipient of spiritual information then we continue to do what we enjoy. For me, if I see results then it is encouragement to do it even better especially if there is demand from those that need it and feel blessed and touched by the shared experience. After all, it is a shared experience. The more one needs spiritual help the more reliable the results should be, and therefore, the less one needs a reading, the less reliable the information or message will be. If the person expecting a reading doesn't need the results, something tends to block or weaken the reception in my opinion.

I have never intended to offend people but when bits of relevant, spiritual information resonate as clear as a bell, then something instantaneously prompts me to confirm it immediately with the recipient. When it just *feels* right, it's what is called in the spiritual business as 'The Knowing'. Its relevance and importance is almost as if one is dictating and obliged to pass the information on.

True, there may not always be a full cohesive message at all. As in my teacher friend Helen's case, when asked 'what is the event that happened concerning oranges?' and her son immediately bursts into laughter to tell his mother he had a fight in the classroom with oranges. They then often put the pieces together to complete or confirm the story. In my opinion they are the missing link for the reader. Not everything may be known –just the salient points.

A spirit seems to know what pieces of relevant information will stimulate or even jog their memory for sure! I know there are those that may disagree with me and classify the incidences as more telepathic but there is a difference here. If all of my experiences were purely just psychic or telepathic, then that would be using solely my own ability – but clairvoyance of the spiritual essence is help from beyond our own physical dimension for which one can receive quite astounding information. This information can be highly personal having only been known by the recipient and nobody else.

However, I can give one example of psychic intuition: Whilst at school in the work place I was walking to lunch with a female teaching colleague, Amy, who was a new member of staff. I felt a surge of calm and peacefulness around her. This prompted me to ask her if she meditated on a regular basis. She confirmed that she did indeed meditate regularly. By standing in the proximity of her aura we can assume this simple example of picking up vibes. In my view, this was evidently not passed on by spirit and therefore not mediumship.

It may seem surprising but for a long period of time I didn't meditate. I am still one of those that find it uncomfortable to have the discipline to sit still for endless periods of time, as some others do in spiritualism and the psychic profession. I hadn't been meditating in any great intensity prior to my teaching classes and was still able to receive spiritual information at that time. However, I do avoid TV, noisy music and radio as I feel it can only hinder the solace and spiritual equilibrium of the mind's psyche and stability if we spend too much time with it.

I recommend just for a while, to sit and relax find a quiet spot, switch off your TV or radio, put on some relaxing music go with the flow or take a walk in the park or countryside. Head to a lake or coast or other waterway and as you visualise and expand on your thoughts, reflect on your life –look at that tree up close, the rugged bark, beautiful plant or butterfly and all its natural wonder, listen to the stream of water coming from the nearby brook and breathe in the scent of those flowers. This of course, is only realistic if you can get the chance to be in this environment. The alternative is to use visualizing techniques but you can't compete with real surroundings in my opinion.

Of course, there are a myriad of CD's to reproduce this effect but given the chance, I relish the real physical world and to be able to physically touch it. Just as like some psychics like to touch old buildings and old trees, some which have been here long before we have. They've occupied more history than we could imagine and are still standing.

Switching off from the physical hustle and bustle of everyday life for a moment, you too may begin to tune in and link up with our other consciousness that is always waiting to be stirred. We can raise our consciousness onto another level therefore encouraging the other dimension to lift the veil to be absorbed in small steps. Once activated it never leaves. Just one typical example is my spirit photography evidence and orb phenomena. But what means more than anything to me is that I have truly had the chance to experience a spiritual world, which some others believe is non-existent.

For this continuing experience, I am extremely grateful. It is true that a large part of my psychic awareness became enhanced through teaching students. Being exposed to a greater number of people to communicate with increased the amount of spiritual experiences. The influx of students and rotation of classes was a bit like a hotel system –they check-in and checkout once a course has been completed. So, the volume of spiritual contact coming through would naturally be significant if any loved ones had passed over and were concerned for their wellbeing. This was also true of the teaching staff turnover – yet more people from a multitude of different backgrounds, nationalities and cultures to work with.

It had taken me quite some time to believe not only in myself that there really is another parallel, spiritual world but also to defend and protect from the barrage of 'flat earth' believers and cynics. There will always be those who are always quick to ridicule or attack others who do believe something less tangible or explainable in scientific terms. This maybe because they themselves can't touch, feel or experience it to the degree some of us have and are able to do so for one reason or another. This cynicism is in stark contrast with those of us who have indeed truly been on the receiving end of the spiritual spectrum – i.e. clairvoyant, psychic and other paranormal experiences.

During my time as a teacher and in one college, as an assistant head of department, there may have been the occasional student that was shocked, but by and large if they were, my messages were disguised as just unusual questions and they were normally taken light-heartedly but all in good fun.

Whilst walking home late one evening, I passed a small castle in The UK and discovered this image after I took the photo. Some have told me it resembles a Knight on horseback but opinions vary.

I took this photo on an outside cabin. It was a favourite place for spirit and unusual images to appear.

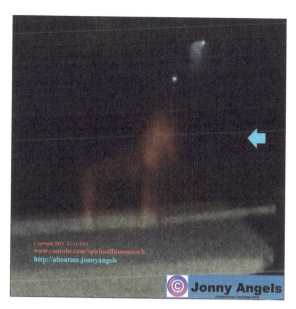

I wasn't sure if this looked like a Unicorn or not. Whatever, this unusual anomaly should not have been there at the time.

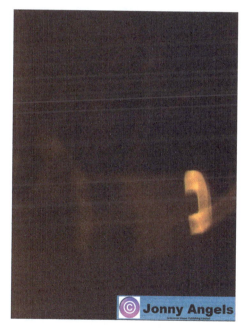

I call this my 'telephone from heaven' image. I have no explanation or other suitable description for it.

This is a photo where I actually asked for some 'action' to occur around a specific flower pot. The result was this.

The author, Jonny Angels in Ulan Bator, The capital city of Mongolia

More faces appear on request on the outdoor cabin

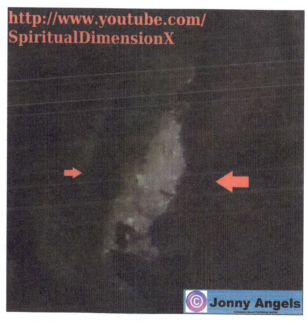

I photographed this head-face image in an old train tunnel in Wales, UK

The author, out and about with the orbs —It's neither snow nor moisture. Taken in the clean air of the countryside.

Experimenting with orbs again.

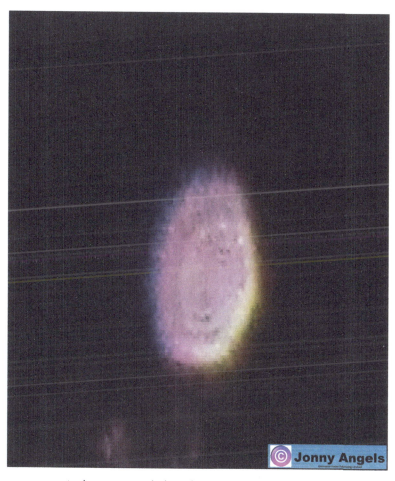

At the time I took this photo, there was a distinct face inside the orb

Chapter 17

Classroom Reflections

I repeatedly reminded my students – the world is not really what it seems, what we understand or perceive it to be and certainly, if we only ever remain focused on the physical world then we will never see the wider picture. In effect, the spirit world is not tangible and therefore cannot be measured in this dimension. These rules do not apply with the spiritual and psychic world, as it is not physical matter we are dealing with, as it cannot be detected by the human physical senses.

This is problematic as science doesn't offer any reasonable help in understanding the non-physical world. It simply is not compatible. Science has always been concerned with what it can measure or detect and in effect, views our world by deeming the physical as something we inhabit and the end result of an evolutionary process. But I firmly believe they are both inter-linked.

Periodically, I sit back and reminisce, reflecting on my own spiritual development. I recall the various people I have come across in the numerous places of work, friendship and study that I have encountered in such a short span of time during my personal awakening decade from teen to adult; All of these, from a multitude of cultures, religions, nationalities ages and backgrounds. They are in effect, souls like each one of us and on a journey, however fraught with obstacles and learning experiences along the way. And whether it may be teacher or psychic, clairvoyant or medium I will always just feel the humble me who stumbled across this other dimension. It was because I had an innate passion and fervent curiosity to know and experience more of what is really out there.

Looking back over the years, I am aware of how the course of my life has been guided and gently steered to where I am today despite me attempting to steer it elsewhere. I am sure I am not the only one who has felt this happening in their own lives. At times I have felt it to be how just like others may feel, as in a small boat being pulled out in a strong tide without navigation. We may disagree with it and argue why it could not have been the way we had truly wanted it. Perhaps Karma does make sense.

I believe that without the psychic experience, being a 'sensitive', which contributed to such problems in my childhood, I would not have had the determination or courage to change direction to go beyond my own culture and home country like a nomadic soul searching for a purpose. What was the other driving force? For me, it may have been the inner desire to do something more adventurous than remain at home in another monotonous job. It may also be in Karmic terms, the spiritual force that propelled me to experience something which has shaped and made me far more informed about the world outside. However, we all have our own paths. If I hadn't received this spiritual push, I would never have been able to utilize an inborn gift. I would also never have pursued with my career in education and exploration of other cultures that has given my life more meaning and fulfilment in a profound spiritual way. I hope you will be able to experience it too and no doubt many of you already have who are reading this.

Since the recent completion of this book I had come to experience, and later experiment with the phenomenon that we call 'Orbs' or Spirit orbs. In many cases this can often be spirit of round-shaped light forms, which appear in our photographs or on video, some being clearer with flash using digital cameras and some without. Immediately following a return trip to the

UK and just prior to my further mediumship development course at a famous College for spiritualism in Essex, near London I bought a new camera.

Actually, I had the sudden urge to buy a new digital camera. I hadn't set out to look for orbs or unusual shapes and lights. Following a consistent pattern of orbs appearing in my photos, I decided to experiment. I wanted to see if the skeptics and more scientific-minded people were right or wrong – that orbs were just pollen, dust or moisture drops. Nearly all my photos for my initial experiment were taken within 12–24 seconds of each consecutive shot but no more than six on each shoot.

I feel some of my photos are unexplainable by science and as a result of my experiments I placed several videos online for all to see at that time. I am not the only witness and the phenomenon seems to be increasing. Do we think that dust, pollen and moisture can be called at will to locate where you ask and show human and animal faces? Well that is what I attempted to rule out in some of my photos. Something else is certainly going on here.

Even NASA has shown an interest in this phenomenon – but then again, they are scientists and so will be examining it from that perspective. I have been able to demonstrate in many photos, proof that the orbs and spirit exist although of course now, this is not new with the abundance of reported orb activity for many to catch on camera. However, I noticed how my experiments developed into images of actual ghost/spirit faces and in some cases, full-body images appearing consistently during my spirit photography sessions. This was also documented on video. Many are experiencing and able to produce this and it is thought by some that a spiritual and cosmic veil is lifting allowing our unconscious mind to be more receptive.

Whereby previously, they would have been simply experiments, now it is substantial, unexplained evidence through the sheer volume of material available. It is also said that amongst the phenomena there are also ghost entities, people who have died but still exist amongst us, but not able to escape from their negative past memories. I would also go one step further and say some didn't move on due to being so emotionally attached to their original surroundings, therefore resisting. It could be just more accessible for them to show up with the rapid technology and equipment we have available. Another more recent experience, I was returning home through the isolated country lanes, as the night was getting darker quickly. I had just been to a spiritualist church and therefore, being aware that I tend to be open and sensitive to spirit, I decided to ask my angels to protect me on the way back home through the country lanes and dark woods. On arriving at the mid point of my journey, I reached an old church where I took some photos above it into the darkness of the late evening sky. Later I checked my camera and noticed two angel looking beings (pink), hovering in the air. One seemed to be holding a wand or some kind of attachment! The images were blurry but scientifically should not be there.

My personal favourite photo consists of several piercing, white lights rotating around our flowerpot in the back garden. It's significant because I had asked spirit to "do something special by the flower pot" right at that time. It's as if they were in harmony and dancing to the nursery rhyme 'a ring of roses' with an angelic presence. Another photo, I held out my arms to reach out to these orbs of light to position directly above me. I asked for some kind of communication as an experiment to establish intelligence and as evidence, received a positive response on camera. But then we have to determine what 'evidence' is and whether science can ever actually prove it.

Meanwhile, no matter how much we avoid the topic of death; nearly all of us will end up at least six feet under unless we are in the furnace as an alternative choice. At least our bodies will. Keeping the notion in mind that everything is temporary here in this physical existence, it's always best to maintain awareness that we are spiritual beings with an afterlife. As Descartes the French Philosopher once said in his philosophical statement – 'I think, therefore I am'. Our consciousness has to exist somewhere even outside the body and there are plenty of cases demonstrating that.

Through my spiritual and psychic communications, I have witnessed and been an active part of what some may call mysterious experiences. Along with the abundance of reincarnation cases that so many others have encountered and have been documented, I made up my mind a long time ago about something more profound happening in this universe. I hope you will also be able to share the experience and realise the truth. I know many of you already have.

* Names and identifying details including some locations have been changed to protect the privacy of individuals.

Bibliography

More Voices in My Ear Doris Stokes, Linda Dearsley Macdonald, 5 Oct 1985.

Imagine (Song) John Lennon 1971, Apple.

René Descartes 31 March 1596 – 11 February 1650 French philosopher.

(French: Je pense, donc je suis; I think, therefore I am.)

Lightning Source UK Ltd.
Milton Keynes UK
UKOW07f2256211214

243491UK00010B/48/P